INSPIRING LEADERSHIP IN
RETAIL & RESTAURANT
DEVELOPMENT

Life Lessons and Shared Inspiration from our
Industry's Top Thought Leaders

A Compendium
by Grace Daly

Grand Street Publishing®

New York

Grand Street Publishing
One Penn Plaza #6220
New York, NY 10119

Daly, Grace
Inspiring Leadership in Retail & Restaurant Development:
Life Lessons and Shared Inspiration from our
Industry's Top Thought Leaders

Cover & page design by Perseus-Design.com

ISBN: 978-0-9828114-3-6
Printed in the United States

Contents

Acknowledgements

My heartfelt gratitude to our sponsors:

American Signcrafters
D.F. Pray General Contractors
HAFELE America Co.
Interstate Signcrafters
Pioneer Properties
RD Weis Companies
The Resicom Group

Thank you for believing in our project. You have given this book wings, allowing it to grow and share its stories and discussions of leadership and inspiration. You make all the difference in moving this industry forward.

Dedication

This book is dedicated to all the men and women in our brick-and-mortar development world who create the client experience and drive sales.

Thank you for designing, building and maintaining our stores and restaurants to ensure that they are safe, functional, brand-protected and, most of all, inviting to the millions of clients that shop and dine with us each and every day.

You all rock.

Introduction

When I first set out to implement this book project, my goal was to understand how our industry thought leaders operate, what drives them and how they inspire their teams. What I've learned is far greater than I can possibly capture in this introduction. I've learned of fun experiences and adventures, as well as growing pains, heartaches and challenges that ultimately shine the light of authenticity on who we are, who we wish to be and who we may become. I've learned of a group of people who are authentic to the core and possess this intrinsic energy—a genuine drive to help others learn and grow in their paths, as well.

It is my hope that you will not only enjoy this collection of stories and interview chats as much as I've had the pleasure of working with each of the coauthors, but that you will also discover this interconnected energy resonating in each and every one of us. This is the energy that emanates from the source of abundance and pure love for our industry, ourselves and each other.

CHAPTER 1

Losing My Hero

By Carl Behler

————————◆◆◆————————

I knew eventually that it would happen; I received the phone call early evening on February 5, 2008. My sister called from Charlotte to let me know that Dad was back in the hospital—his third time in about a year, only this time it was serious and he did not want to go through another major surgery. I wanted to immediately leave Maryland and rush to be with my mom and sister and her family there at the hospital, but they talked me into waiting until the doctors consulted. We had been though this so many times, only each time he defied medical logic and completely recovered.

The tone in my mom's voice the next morning on the 6th said it all: "Carl, Dad is slipping away and you should come." That was the longest seven-hour drive ever had. I had been through at least five or six major surgeries with Dad, two of them open-heart surgeries. I have seen him at his strongest and his weakest, and watched his health deteriorate, so I am questioning how much more can he take. When I walked in his room at the ICU he grinned from ear to ear and said, "Carl... You are here." That evening after my family left to eat and get some rest after 24 hours by his side, I sat there with my hero, reliving in my own head our life together: the good, the bad, and the ugly. The doctor told us that he would not survive another surgery, and yet to not have one would be fatal: An intestinal blockage was poisoning his system. Through the morphine and fever, he let me know even without words that I was his beloved oldest son, a man after his own heart, and he was so proud of me. We did not talk a lot; we didn't need to. We had nothing between us to say, "I'm sorry," for or to forgive each other for. We were up to date; holding hands and looking in each other's eyes was enough. We were living in the precious acceptance of the situation, the moment, and each other. I have never felt love like I did in that moment—pure love and no fear. We both let go; he wanted to move on to his Father, and I wanted him to not suffer any more. I silently asked God to take him home, and He obliged.

A little after midnight the morning of the 8th, my dad slipped into a coma, and shortly thereafter he was declared brain-dead. I made the difficult call to my mom and family. He lasted another couple of hours and then peacefully passed away. Later that day, I realized what a blessing this experience was for me, the black sheep of our family. Even now, over five years later, it continues to shape and mold me, and has become an inspiration for change in my life.

The Early Years

From the age of nine, I worked for Dad on Saturdays during school season and five days a week in the summer. His carpet, flooring, and ceramic tile business was booming in those days, and I loved watching him and his guys lay tile and carpet and install ceramic in the showers, bathrooms, and floors of new homes. I was in awe of how they could cut with their knives, spread adhesive with a trowel, and grout the new ceramic; I wanted to be like them. One day, Dad let me mix up a batch of cement mortar in the front dirt yard of the new split-level home we were working in, a mixture of sand, cement, and water. I amazed them all until I had to shovel it into a wheelbarrow and push it up into the front door on two 2x12s side-by-side into the front door. I spilled the entire load onto the dirt, and they all laughed so hard... I was hurt, and I ran and hid, my pride wounded. Dad came with a hug and assured me that they laughed because they too had done the same thing a time or two and I get an "A" for effort. Where I felt I had failure they saw success!

I worked for Dad until after I graduated from high school, and it was during that time I fell in love with creativity. I liked the fact that we could transform a bare new home in two or three days into a thing of beauty with new carpet, Formica, ceramic, and flooring. This is where I learned the tools of my trade. As a child I was blessed with an artistic talent, while in high school I learned that I had considerable hand-eye coordination for architectural drafting, art, music, design, and writing. After I graduated in the summer of 1970, I applied for a drafting job with McCrory Stores in downtown York, Pennsylvania. Much to my surprise, I was hired and was put on the drafting board working under some really great designers and architects. I seemed to thrive in this environment in which perfection, artistic talent with a drafting pencil, agility, and speed was in demand. The process and art of communicating a vision through drawing and then visually creating the procedure for building that vision still amazes and intrigues me.

Later that year the "call of the wild" possessed me, and I felt guitar playing, writing songs and poetry, and traveling was going to be my calling in life; this was the early 1970s, after all. It seemed better than all of the rules of no long hair, being at work on time, and so on. I lived in a barn in the country with several other like-minded folks and had a blast for two summers and a long winter. Eventually I moved to California to pursue my dreams, but returned broke and disappointed two years later as a prodigal son appearing on the front porch of my parents' house. Then I began my over-the-road long-haul truck driving career. At the time, I wanted nothing but call of the wild adventure without responsibility. Truck driving, along with sporadically working for Dad, carried me through the '70s, wide-eyed, idealistic, and aimless. I ended up in South Texas in early 1980 working in a shipbuilding yard first as a loftsman, a welder, and then a marine draftsman. It was there that I was reunited with my love for drafting and design. When the shipbuilding company folded, I applied for a drafting position with a fast food burger chain and began my career in restaurant development. I managed the design and drafting department for the company and eventually ventured into construction management. I fell in love with the restaurant industry, and still am today. There is something profoundly different about a dining experience as compared to a pure retail shopping experience. To me, restaurants evoke a response from the five senses, and what you take away is in your belly and not in a shopping bag.

In late 1988 I returned to Pennsylvania and went to work back at McCrory Stores, only this time as a seasoned design manager for their restaurant division, working with some very talented people. Traveling back to Texas in 1991, I started a successful restaurant development consulting firm, and coincidentally the fast food chain where I learned my trade was my first and largest client until I sold the company several years later. It was there that I learned I was able to apply my design skills and develop entire sets of CDs for constructing a new restaurant, every sheet with my own hands—a labor of love that built my confidence in my ability to sell myself and my ideas. From there I went on to become the director of construction for a national fast food drive-in restaurant chain, my first of many leadership positions in retail and restaurant development From the mid-1990s through 2003, I worked with several national restaurant and retail organizations' in-store development at various management levels. I found through the years that great leaders are not made; you either are on or you're not.

In 2003 I began working as an "outsourced CM" for an up-and-coming fast casual restaurant company. It was sort of a step backwards for me; however, the very high potential in the brand and the culture and people of the company intrigued me. They had outstanding food, very simple methods, top-performing people, and an excellent financial model. In 2005 I was promoted to the position of development director and added real estate responsibilities to the design and construction knowledge I already had. Today our company has become the most successful fast casual restaurant company in the US, with over 1300 restaurants nationwide and several in the London, Paris, Toronto.

How did I get to this wildly challenging and successful place? I subscribe to these thoughts: I never expected it, and I do not deserve it, but I accept it and am deeply grateful for it.

Through the years I learned many life lessons from my dad, Charlie. He was a simple man, very humble with the attitude of a servant, a man of deep spiritual faith, and he lived it. He was a man of honor to his God, family, and country. He did not finish high school, had no college education, and had no interest in becoming wealthy or famous. Dad had convictions and could tell you what they were and why he believed in them. Dad and Mom were strict with me; my brother and sister and I am grateful to this day for that. My Dad was my hero and taught me valuable lessons on life, living, and love.

After Dad passed away on February 8, 2008, I was asked by my mom to speak on behalf of our family at a memorial service at the church I attended where I grew up. What an honor it was to accept that and to be able to see and hear how many people my dad touched in very positive ways. I was able to share with everyone some of the profound life lessons I learned from my dad, Charlie. As I reflected on my dad's legacy and my own successes and failures over the years, I have developed several important thoughts that help me stay grounded. Applying these in any situation seems to attract others to me, and I am able to share with them the personal lessons that guide me and have helped me become a leader, and through this I am able to positively affect the lives of others.

Life lessons from Charlie

Keep a Clean Slate: Remember in grade school when we all had to take turns in washing the blackboard so it was fresh and ready for the teacher the next day? I try to apply that principal to my life daily as I reflect upon my day. If I harmed or offended someone, I promptly try and make amends. Did I do the right thing? If not, how can I make it right? I have learned from experience that I do not carry the weight of guilt well at all. Having a clear conscience and having a clean slate with my God, others, and myself allows me to focus on the present than rather then the past. Then I can live without fear and can freely forgive and forget. This is true freedom.

Watch Your Buttons: You've heard the expression: "They really pushed my buttons, so I got mad." I have learned that if others push my buttons, it is because I have them sticking out! It amazes me how on two different days driving the same route into Washington, DC, I can be hot as a hornet when other drivers annoy me one day, and yet the next day I am calm, cool, and collected. Did the road or traffic change? No, my attitude did and my buttons were not sticking out. If I am living on the correct beam, I cannot be easily offended because I am not dwelling on self. The times when my overinflated view of self is in the forefront are the times when I allow others to push my buttons, and usually the result is not good.

Don't Hide Your Scars: Dad used to get a kick out of showing his scars from his two heart surgeries. He'd tell us that he feels a special connection with other heart surgery patients as a result of their common scars. We are all human and have very real scars: emotional, physical, and spiritual. I lived for years trying to hide and cover up my scars so that I could be perceived as successful, lovable, and perfect. Along the way though perhaps I have denied others the opportunity to relate to me. Being open with my weaknesses, I become human and approachable, allowing others to see the real me. Exposing my struggles, foibles, and scars means that I am not ashamed of them; they are a part of what has shaped me, and that has value. As Popeye said, "I yam what I yam!" Let others know that you are human and just like them; expose your wounds and scars, you'll be amazed at how others will be attracted to you.

Laugh at Yourself: Some days I take myself so seriously that I fool myself into believing that I am perfect. Wrong! I am a human being with real feelings, faults, and struggles in life. Life is not a serious matter, and it is not an entitlement; it can fade away in a moment. Happy people laugh—no, I mean really laugh—and when you laugh, others will join you. Since I have to live, why not live happily, and laugh? Live, laugh, and love!

Don't worry about tomorrow's worries: If I am living in yesterday or in tomorrow, I am ruining my today. Tomorrow will have its own worries, and I have no control over them today. Living in the "now" and "here" means that I am living "nowhere" but in the moment. The reality is that I have absolutely no control over tomorrow, yet I fool myself into believing that I do. The more I let go of that, the less stress and worry I have, and the easier my life becomes; it's so simple, yet hard to do.

Accept Acceptance Gracefully: This concept has been the most difficult thing for me to put into practice in daily living. After living in the corporate world for so many years, where climbing the ladder means everything, it is tough to accept anything without having to earn it. The concept of being acceptable without a scorecard or rating is foreign at best to most of us. I believe that as humans we desire two things in life more than anything else: love and acceptance. I, for one, have expended much energy and resources seeking these two things, at times even to my own detriment. I laugh at the way my false self occasionally says, "You shouldn't have!" when someone gives me an unexpected gift, instead of a simple heartfelt thank-you. To accept acceptance means that first I must accept myself as I am. This requires an honest inventory of my strengths and weaknesses and the desire to change as needed. It also helps to know "who" I am and "whom" I belong to. Brandon Manning, my favorite author, once said, "If God had a refrigerator, your picture would be on it." What an incredible expression of love and acceptance that I use to ground myself.

When I reflect on my life and consider how I started as a small-town country boy with no formal education, I am humbled and amazed. Each day I try to tell someone part of my story or expose a "scar" in hopes that they will find a bit of inspiration. Everyone has a story behind their story that is worthwhile getting to know. Try it—it might work for you, as well.

About Carl

Within the retail and restaurant industries, Carl has spent 32 years refining his development expertise in real estate, design, and construction. Carl began his design career as an "old school" architectural draftsman at McCrory Stores in York, PA in 1970.

Through those early years, Carl's life experiences took him through a career in music, over the road long haul truck driving, operating his father's flooring/ceramic tile/carpet business, a naval draftsman at a ship building yard, and finally back to architectural design in the early 80's. Landing at Whataburger, Inc. in Corpus Christi, TX Carl was introduced to his first restaurant drafting and design position in the restaurant industry. In 1991 Carl formed Restaurant Designs, Inc in Bedford, TX and provided turnkey restaurant design, permitting, and construction management services for several restaurant companies specializing in major restaurant renovations and new store prototype design. After selling the company in 1993 Carl joined Sonic Drive-In and became their first Director of Construction. From 1997 through 2003 Carl held Director level store development positions with Carrols Corporation, Noodle Kidoodle, Zany Brainy, and HMS Host. In 2003 Carl became an out sourced Construction Manager for Chipotle Mexican Grill and joined them as a full time employee in early 2004. From August 2005 through August 2012 Carl was a Development Director at Chipotle leading the NE Development Team and their real estate, design, and construction management professionals in new store development. In August of 2012 Carl was named Development Director – Special Projects and is exclusively dedicated to Chipotle's new Shophouse Southeast Asian Kitchen as well as other special projects.

Carl currently serves on the RestaurantPoint Advisory Board with other influential restaurant leaders who share their experience and lend support for the benefit of the restaurant industry. Carl and his family reside in Annapolis, MD.

CHAPTER 2

Being Worth Following

By John Fairclough

When asked why they love their jobs, people cite the challenge of their work as the single biggest reason. People who can solve problems and put their skills and talent to use draw personal satisfaction in the feeling of accomplishment. Digging deeper, however, we find that it's not the specific tasks or challenges that boost job satisfaction, but the leadership team in place that helps the team find success.

People who report that they love their jobs usually cite a great boss as a main contributing factor. When searching for challenging, meaningful work, a manager can enhance or diminish the experience. A great leader has the ability to boost influence within a team. Empowering individuals helps to tap their own potential. A poor leader that only influences through coercion, demands or threats is assembling a disconnected team without a shared interest in common goals. Teams that produce from a sense of responsibility and engagement typically outperform the teams working merely out of obligation.

Building an engaged team starts with a leader who is influential rather than authoritative. A mediocrity gap is created when leaders have high authority but low influence. A team under a dictatorship might perform grudgingly, without understanding why a task is important and how it connects back to the overall strategic goal. However, without the insight as to how his or her role helps define the overall success of the organization, it's easy for the employee to become disconnected, then apathetic. The "because I say so" management style only serves to promote confusion and resentment.

Ever find yourself flipping through TV channels and if Braveheart pops up you'll stop and watch a bit, even if it's in the middle of the movie? Why do we love this story so much? What is it about the character's "Freedom!" battle cry that we find so compelling and heroic? The character is a Scotsman without title or money that finds himself, at first somewhat reluctantly, leading a rebellion against English tyranny. He didn't have the military authority to enlist soldiers or press upon others to fight. Yet, people naturally gravitated toward his leadership. His men are inspired to fight against incredible odds.

He had a level of influence greater than his authority. A manager may have the authority to draft someone to a task, but it's all about obligation. True influence, by contrast, occurs when leaders inspire others to act from a sense of responsibility. Great leaders don't force others; they are subservient to the cause, and win their team's commitment.

A team led through influence rather than authority can answer yes to three critical questions about their leader:

- Does my leader know what he or she doing?

- Can I trust this leader?

- Does my leader care about me personally?

No one wants to follow an incompetent manager. An effective leader can help others accomplish their goals. In order for the employee to meet the goal, the leader first needs to define exactly what success looks like for that person and align his or her goals with the big picture. Success needs to be defined in clear, specific language with concrete objectives and outcomes. Vague, ambiguous goals leave the individual in a state of anxiety. If success isn't defined, then the default is translated as perfection—but perfection isn't always possible or even desirable.

A person could waste countless hours doing unnecessary tasks that have no direct link to any real, identifiable goal. How does this happen? When no clear direction is provided, the default mindset becomes: "Since I have no idea where the margin for error exists, I'd better make sure I've crossed all my t's and dotted all my i's." The problem is that crossing ALL t's and dotting ALL i's might not be necessary and could actually be costly and counterproductive. Efficiency doesn't always equal effectiveness. We can do something efficiently, but that doesn't mean that it contributes to accomplishing our goals.

When a team meets or exceeds a clearly outlined goal that supports the overall strategy, that's when those feelings of personal satisfaction for a job well done really kick in. A good leader sets expectations then provides feedback on how progress can be adjusted or refined to meet the goal.

When situations occur that are unique, difficult, or counterintuitive to goals, that's when the effective leader needs to communicate clearly with the team. Support can be boosted during adversity if the reasons why something needs to be done and the action steps needed are clearly shared and explained. The delegator's responsibility is to ensure that the recipient is successful with his or her objective. Thus, communication that demonstrates a firm comprehension of not only the goal, but also situations that threaten the goal and the opportunities to prevail, reinforce belief in the leader's competence.

Building upon this trust, there may be times when quick, decisive action is called for and the leader can explain the reasons at a later time. A history of communicating clearly and courageously will allow the leader to draw upon previous deposits into the relationship. In effect, the leader will be able to say, "Trust me—let's do this now, and I'll explain later." Because of the history established with the team as an effective and courageous communicator, the leader will still be able to rally the team to the cause.

A team asking themselves whether or not they trust a leader is defining that person's character. A leader can't be effective and commit others to the cause if his or her character is in question. Effective and decisive communication, especially during difficult times, becomes currency that can be spent to earn a team's trust. Taking time to explain the purpose of why a task needs to be completed, in addition to explaining the specifics of what to do, is an important tool. Communicating in a way that dispels the threat of hidden agendas or withheld information becomes a leader's track record of "doing what they say and saying what they do."

No one wants to work for Jekyll and Hyde, despite how great the job description might sound. A history of behavior that is consistent with the company's core values reinforces trust. The expectation will be reinforced that what the company wants and believes actually exists in the day-to-day interactions between leaders and workers. By demonstrating ethics and consistent objectivity in tough decisions, leaders set the example of upheld standards.

Leaders can build trust through training, especially when used to promote the individual's best interests as well as the interests of the organization. Providing consistent, timely feedback helps people transfer what they've learned into real application and refine their own effectiveness. Insightful training has an objective to connect the dots for a person's role and how his or her contribution relates back to the broader focus of the company goals.

Being forthright is another key to building trust. If I tell you about something that I did wrong that you might not otherwise have found out, I am able to demonstrate that I am trustworthy and that I care about you. Consider if I borrowed your car and spilled coffee in the back seat. If I brought it in to be cleaned and it came out looking great, would you still want to know that I had spilled the coffee? Most people would answer yes. This is because most people want to be informed about what is going on with things they are connected to. Now consider what would happen to my trustworthiness if I borrowed your car again, and so did three other people, and you got your car back with a coffee stain in the back seat, and you asked me if I had caused it and I said no. Would you believe me? Most people would because I had already demonstrated being forthright and truthful when I did not need to. My word and my trustworthiness were established with you. (Though you might not want to loan me your car anymore...)

Why would a team follow a leader that thinks of them as dispensable and irrelevant? The short answer is: They wouldn't. When workers feel that a leader doesn't care about them, this usually occurs due to a lack of communication. This erodes a person's confidence that a leader cares about him or her as a person that has individual goals and needs. Leaders who take time to explain and engage in active dialogue with a team demonstrate concern on a personal level. A great leader understands that people feel self-worth when those in leadership roles invest their time to communicate and listen.

The opportunity for mutual admiration and even compatibility can be built when leaders take time to interact and engage with the team. Focusing on the individual and connecting with the human behind the computer screen become an investment in the relationship. Sharing experiences and being vulnerable are things that the leader can initiate to strengthen this relationship. Intrinsic rewards beyond a paycheck become possible when leaders demonstrate appropriate compassion.

When someone feels valued as a person and not just as an employee, a culture develops that goes beyond money. Employees make a conscious decision to stay and contribute, and can even be encouraged to follow their leader to a different organization or endeavor.

The most efficient leaders can be completely ineffective at motivating a team and driving results. Despite what traditional business theories might claim, these two concepts—efficiency and effectiveness—are not always connected. Effective leaders build teams by building up individuals. Managers manage things: the budgets, the production schedule, the charts and operation tasks. Effective leaders lead people. They encourage and inspire, empathize, evaluate and reward. While managers can be completely efficient and do things right, leaders are effective by doing the right thing.

About John

John Fairclough founded The Resicom Group and has helped it evolve from a local construction company into an international provider of facility maintenance services. John lives in the Chicago area with his wife and two daughters and regularly tries to sell the idea that the family should move to California. Each winter his argument gains momentum, only to be thwarted by spring when he suddenly finds himself back at square one.

John has a knack for understanding what it takes to become his team's favorite employer, his vendor's favorite client, and his client's favorite vendor. This ability has sped the success of his team. It's kind of ironic that the person who operates behind the scenes to empower others to be successful would end up becoming one of the youngest people ever inducted into the Chicago Area Entrepreneur Hall of Fame. He believes he was able to sneak in because they were trying to hit their quota of people that wear jeans and t-shirts to work that carry an orange back pack.

Naturally curious, he spends his time developing better questions to find the "uncommon sense" of a situation. By improving his questions, he has been able to create better answers to the challenge of developing people, evolving their processes, and protecting the value delivered to clients. His office looks like a library, but the word on the street is that the books are just for show. For now, he would like to keep you guessing.

CHAPTER 3

Interview Chat

with Lori Bonin

Grace: Lori, where did you grow up and how big was your family?

Lori: I was born in Detroit and lived there until I was eight years old. I am the oldest of three girls; my youngest sister and I are 16 years apart. I live in Minneapolis. From a very young age, I learned that life is about blessings and that flexibility and agility are at times more important than focus and structure.

Grace: Do you remember the first store you shopped at or the first restaurant you ate in?

Lori: As a child, one of the first stores I shopped at was Kresgee – like K-mart. I have memories of my parents and how they financed our purchases by placing some of the items on a lay away plan. A fond memory and big deal was the family shopping and then eating out at the Hudson's Department Store in Detroit. The restaurant was on an upper floor that overlooked the court of the mall. It was cool to eat out in this fancy restaurant where we dressed our best, meaning my mom did not allow us to wear jeans.

Grace: What schools did you attend? How did you get started in the industry?

Lori: I attended public schools in Minneapolis, Southwest High School and then the University of St. Thomas for business, with a concentration in accounting. I started as a CPA for six years with Ernst & Young. Target was one of my first clients. I was called by a staff accountant at Target who encouraged me to apply for a role and ended up being her new boss! I started with Target in Finance. When I came to a crossroads and decided to do property management for Target's 600 stores, I loved the change! My finance role was great – but I love my job because there is a direct impact to the customer. Each day is different! I truly believe you can create strategic plans in this industry, despite the fact much of it is reactionary. For example, you can have all the plans in place for a hurricane - but you still have to react to that.

Grace: Which was your favorite job?

Lori: Property Manager in the facilities management industry. I worked with Dayton Hudson, Marshall Fields, Mervyns in addition to Target. I was involved when they sold those retailers. I've been exclusively with Target for about 6 years now. My current job is my favorite. It's more related to the journey and culture change I've been working with the team on the last 4 years; seeing the impact of the transformation. I've loved all the elements of the other jobs – but this one affects both team and culture.

Grace: As an industry thought leader, what do you think we're doing great in this industry? What are we excelling at?

Lori: Innovation, really continuing to provide transparency to the significance and importance of facilities management to the overall business. We've been better collaborators between retailers and vendors in an approach of "let's all win together". There will always be bad eggs – but a lot less. I've been in the industry for 14 years. At an earlier point in time – it was old school; there were a lot fewer women in our industry. Some vendors may have been padding purchase orders. Now, there's much more credibility to the industry for our business. Lots of the innovation falls into energy – clear returns on investment and even for companies to get behind that. The industry needs more innovation in strategic asset management. Understanding our total cost of ownership from design, purchase, construction, maintenance and then replacement.

Grace: What do you think we can improve upon as an industry?

Lori: Where do we prioritize resources? People or technology? In retail it has to be whatever drives the stores sales. We need to do a better job of demonstrating the value and importance of how the impact of facility maintenance has on sales. Specifically, with more online retailers, we need to show every reason why a customer would want to shop in our stores, beyond the product offerings.

Grace: Do you love what you do? How important do you feel it is for a leader – to absolutely love what they do?

Lori: Yes, I'm very passionate about what I do. My guess is the general population does not love what they do. I feel very fortunate to enjoy what I do but what I find is most important is to connect with the culture of the Company. My advice is as a leader – think about what do you really love? What are the elements you love so it can be aligned with what you do, usually that is what you're really good at and you will thrive.

Grace: What are the most important three traits that you feel make up strong leadership?

Lori: It's respect, character and being strategic. Respect is being respectful with all people and genuinely caring for people. Character means really having strong integrity and honesty. Even though we respect and care about people – we need to be honest as hard as it may be. It is foundational to have strong character. The third is being strategic - that's the differential. People have more potential to grow if they are strategic and have strong thought leadership.

Grace: What are the most important three traits that you feel that make up strong teams?

Lori: The first one is trust. Team members need to trust each other. This is the core of it all. The second one is honesty. They need to be very honest and have that open line of communication. The third one ties into respect. Team members need to value each other and each others' strengths.

Grace: What is the most important lesson you've learned in this industry that will help someone else along their career path?

Lori: You need to understand your client and their operations. What is really important is you can influence and leverage that knowledge to show your value and how you can influence and collaborate for decisions that impact the business as a whole.

Grace: If you had to do it all over again – what, if anything, would you do differently?

Lori: One of the main things is I would have probably have taken some time out to be a manager in the stores. This experience would have added to my toolkit so that I could best balance my knowledge of operations and facilities management. From a leadership perspective, I am fortunate to have experience in different situational challenges. Including taking over a turnaround situation, starting up a new area and managing a group taken over from a great leader. These opportunities happened randomly and I would have wanted it to have happened more purposeful; organically as I was developing this experience.

Grace: Who was the most impactful role model or mentor for you? How have they impacted your career? Your life?

Lori: My dad was the primary person to ground me in the area of character. I remember as a kid in high school – around 15 or 16 years old I went to my dad's workplace. My dad had taken over a segment of his company. In the front row of the parking lot – there was a parking sign designated for the CEO but he didn't park there. He told me: "The team knows that sign is coming down – I'm not so busy that I can't walk an extra 20 feet to the front door." This showed his team who he was as a leader and tied into his respect for others.

When I took my current role, working with my team and operations – there was tension. People said I couldn't do it. I had a mentor in Target; he was supportive and reminded me to identify 3 core things I'm going after. Then focus, communicate it to the partners and with the team; communicating regularly; sharing progress. One VP actually told me he didn't think I could do it – but that my communication and focus on developing a strong team supported driving the needed change and he eventually told me he believed in me. It took 18 months to impact that change effectively.

Grace: Are you a role model or mentor for someone else?

Lori: I mentor a handful of people. Generally people that get referred to me are women and they're looking for work/life balance advice, especially since in most families both spouses are working now. They've also sought my help for career guidance. I have conversations with these individuals; sharing my own experiences. I also help them recognize that work life balance is not linear – it's circular. It's how you live your values each day. As an example, I practice my values by volunteering at my kids' school. This ensures I see more of my 10 and 14 year old kids while impacting the community.

Grace: Any last pearls of wisdom to share?

Lori: When I was in finance – and the property management position came up on – there was also another position available. I was approached by my VP for FM who wanted me to join his team. The other position I would have to apply for. I remembered my grandfather's words of advice from his career: "Go where you're loved." Meaning, if you love what you do and you go where you're loved – you will be successful.

About Lori

Lori Bonin is the Vice President of Facilities Management for Target Stores. She started her career with Ernst & Young as a CPA. Lori has held a variety of positions at Target in Finance, Operations and Property Development and is a member of IFMA. She is actively involved in the community and serves as a Treasurer and Board Member of a large non-profit organization in St. Paul, MN. Lori lives in the Twin Cities with her husband and two children.

CHAPTER 4

Finding Your Purpose

By Greg Carpenter

From the beginning of time, mankind has been questioning its purpose. To find the answer, many have turned to religion, others anthroplogy, some to archeology, and a few have even linked us to alien life forms from faraway worlds. Being less a philosopher and more of a realist, I believe that we each have several purposes to play out in our lifetimes; some are centered around family, some religion, while others are career-oriented. I believe that to understand our purposes, we must each define them and even strive to find their origins. It is a really basic question, actually: "Why do we do what we do?"

For the purpose of this discussion, I would like to focus on the aspect of our career purpose. As a child, we were always being asked, "What do you want to be when you grow up?" We would stop for a second and think about all of the exciting opportunities, ranging from astronaut to fireman. I can only think of one person who answered most assuredly, "I'm gonna be a maintenance man when I grow up!" Yes, as sad as that sounds, it was me. To know who I am and to understand my purpose, you must first know where I came from—not geographically, but in terms of the people and events that influenced me in such a way that I was sure of my career destiny. I do not want this to be my autobiography, but my story has relevance that can be used as an example to better understand the people that work on our teams.

When I turned seven years old, I was given a set of open-end wrenches for my birthday. My friends had received bikes, footballs, and other toys on their special days. These would last for a few months and then disappear or be thrown away. But not me—I received tools. This was the start of my very own toolbox. One Saturday morning, I was looking through my Dad's huge tool chest, trying to decide which shiny tool I could "borrow" and put in mine. Those few new wrenches I was given were awfully lonely in that big, shiny new box. As I carefully picked through the drawers, I noticed that his tools had his initials engraved in them. As I looked closer, I found initials that were not his on some of the other tools. I had never noticed this before. I would always just reach in a drawer and grab whatever one I was asked to get when I was the "gofer." It didn't take long before he caught me on one of my shopping trips and asked me what I was doing. To quickly change the subject, I asked him about the initials on the tools and why they weren't all his. We sat down on our official mechanic stools (five-gallon buckets), and he grabbed a few wrenches from one of the drawers. The first one was old and battered. This one, I was told, was used by his grandpa in the coal mines where he worked in the late 1800s. As a seven-year-old, I wasn't interested in an old tool; I wanted a bright, shiny new one and kept looking back at the others left in the drawer. He grabbed another and told me that this one was used by his dad in the gas station where he worked before my dad was even born. Again, "Show me a new one" was all I could think about. The next one I recognized as being his from the initials scratched into the steel. He looked at me and then, without saying a word, he got up and took my new wrenches over to the workbench and engraved my initials into these shiny new pieces. My first reaction was that he just messed up those new pieces of chromed finished steel that I polished almost daily. I even went as far as to ask him why he was doing it; I knew they were mine, and so did he. Then the epiphany (if a seven-year-old is capable of having one)—I started to get it. At that precise moment in time, my purpose was set. I knew what I was going to be when I grew up, because it was what I was in that moment. It was my heritage, my destiny, my duty to pass the torch, so to speak.

My dad worked as a maintenance mechanic in a glass factory for 43 years up until the day he passed away a few years ago. The day after his funeral, I had the emotional task of cleaning out his garage. As one might expect, I got all of his tools and trucked them 1500 miles back to my home. Since that time, many have been sold and others were given to friends and family, but some are destined to remain in my tool chest until the time comes when I'm gone. I made it a point to keep every single tool that had those timeless initials forever engraved in them. They aren't the best ones, the most useful, or the easiest to use. Nevertheless, they hold a prime location in a special drawer in my garage. I often pull some of them out and run my fingers over the worn scratch marks and think of all the machines, cars, bikes and go-carts they have fixed over the years. I imagine the hands, greasy and scuffed up, using them and then carefully, almost lovingly, wiping them off before putting them back in their assigned place in the tool chest.

I didn't choose my career; it chose me. It actually defined who I was and who I was going to be. It just came naturally, like growing up and starting a family. I know that not everyone has this profound defining moment that determines their purpose that guides their career. Some find their purpose when they declare a major in college. Others jump from job to job, hoping to land on that one thing that they enjoy doing. Then there are those who are looking for that elusive position that will bring them fortune and power.

Now that you know my story, stop for a moment and look at your own. As leaders, we have all had people and events that have shaped our careers and guided us to where we are at this point in our lives. Our management styles are delicate combinations of emulation and avoidance. We do the things we like about the leaders we respect, and avoid those things that upset us as subordinates. Take a look back and remember those people and events that influenced you and helped you make the decisions that led you to your current role. Try to understand what made them special and why you allowed them to have such a profound impact on your career. Whether you realized it or not, they were helping you define your purpose. Something they did or said focused your attention and pointed you in a specific direction toward your purpose. It is very important that we understand what brought us to where we are and keeps us motivated to stay the course. Our purpose is more than goals and objectives; it is the driving force that determines the leaders we are—and better yet, the leaders we want to become. At times, it is easy to confuse purpose with ambition. *Webster's Dictionary* defines purpose as "something set up as an object to be attained, the goal or aim of a person: what a person is trying to do or become." Ambition is what drives us to excel or succeed. Consider it this way: Ambition is the drive to win the race, and purpose is knowing that you were born to drive the car.

As important as it is that you understand your purpose, it is equally if not more important that you understand your role in determining other people's purposes. As leaders, we like to think that we have a positive influence on the people that work on our teams. We all need to take a good, often hard, look in the mirror and ask ourselves if we are the leaders that people are trying to imitate or the ones demonstrating what not to do or be like. If you don't know your purpose, the members of your team won't know it, either. If they don't know your purpose, they will create or perceive one for you. You might never know that they have done it—or worse, not know what it is. Their perception of you and your purpose is their reality. Therefore, they have determined who you are and what is important to you without ever asking. Oftentimes, these perceptions are totally false and can be detrimental to your relationship with them and the rest of the team. They will share their perceptions with others, and consequently others will view you in the same manner. Remember, it is up to you to share your purpose with others. Sometimes it is not easy for them to see or understand. All too often, we let our jobs define who we are and thus let others define us. A job title is just that: a description of our job. A title should not describe the person or define who he or she is. I doubt that the CEO of a multinational corporation is the CEO in his household. He is a spouse, a parent, a friend, or the person that cleans up after the dog makes a mess in the house. Getting the point? CEO is the job title, what he does at work—not his purpose. Simply put, purpose is what makes us who we are as human beings and as leaders. We must do our best to understand this, and how our purpose profoundly affects the way we manage our teams. We must allow others to know our purpose and help others define theirs. The key is knowing your purpose, sharing it, and finding purpose in others. Remember, there is always someone looking at you as a leader and expecting you to set the example. Recognize the ones looking to you to help them find their purpose.

About Greg

Greg has been in the Maintenance discipline for over 30 years. He has worked in the textile and non-wovens industry, paper manufacturing, food manufacturing, logistics and restaurant facilities. His resume lists companies including Kimberly-Clark, International Paper, Quaker Oats, Wal-Mart Logistics and Whataburger Restaurants. Greg is currently the Director of Maintenance Services for Whataburger Restaurants and resides in San Antonio, Texas. He leads a team of 135 dedicated and talented Technicians, Field Leaders and Administration staff providing 24/7 equipment and facilities maintenance service to over 650 corporate operated restaurants in 10 states. In his spare time, Greg enjoys cycling in the Texas hill country, scuba diving, classic muscle cars and is a licensed pilot.

CHAPTER 5

Interview Chat

with Jeff Petersen

Grace: Where did you grow up? How big was your family?

Jeff: I grew up on Long Island, born in Elmhurst Queens. Not a big family: one sister, one brother; my dad was NYPD, my mom was stay at home mom then.

Grace: Do you remember the first store you shopped at or the first restaurant you ate in?

Jeff: Woolworth – I remember shopping in the pet department that sold little turtles. When I was old enough to walk to stores – I went to buy candy and Superman comics books at the five and dime in Copiague. As for restaurants – it was Howard Johnsons. Also the first McDonalds was in Babylon by the A&S stores. A&W Rootbeer was another chain. We use to go to Lindenhurst movie theaters for 35 cents then.

Grace: What schools did you attend?

Jeff: I graduated from Massapequa High School then apprenticed 3 years in the sheet metal industry based in NYC. I've earned degrees in: School of hard knocks – degree: Life. School of harder knocks – degree: Survival!

Grace: What was your first job in this niche industry?

Jeff: When I was 16 – I quit school and through my girlfriend's mom who was a secretary there – I went to work for Kal Steinfeld (Jerry Steinfeld's dad) sign company. I worked there for a year, then I went back to school but worked with other local sign companies until I had the opportunity to work with ArtCraft Strauss. I built a lot of spectaculars in Times Square. During that time I also started soliciting on my own. With a pickup truck and ladder, I solicited service calls on my own. I didn't even have a company or insurance set up! I saw where there was neon out, worked out a gig with sign removers to take the old transformers. Then I started the company TJ Signs in 1979.

Grace: Which was your favorite job in this niche industry?

Jeff: When I was more hands on, building the business but still on the bench and in the trucks. It's very gratifying to build something. It's the finished product; some signs are more complicated than others. It's very satisfying getting a big job up in the air, driving away from it and seeing it for the next 20 years. Back in the day we had crazy rigging to get a job done. Today, it's much easier; we would use 2 cranes and a bucket truck. Some of the feats that were accomplished with limited resources was life threatening but it builds character.

Grace: As an industry thought leader, what do you think we're doing great in this industry? What are we excelling in?

Jeff: In the industry – we're keeping up with technology: LEDs has caused neon tubes to disappear over the course of 7 – 10 years. Neon is still serviced as required – but it's outsourced. LEDs are constantly refined to make it more cost effective. In terms of the fabrication of our products – there's computerized folding breaks for intricate sheet metal work and laser cutters. The end user sees the same product – but the technology is better to manufacture. The rage now is the digital signage – big TV screens. Also digital printing is now so affordable and available for frequent changing of the billboard type signage.

Grace: What do you think we can improve upon as an industry?

Jeff: This industry is being regulated to death. We have constraints put on us by municipalities that are prohibitive. Certainly there has to be basic criteria for safety – but more and more ARB (Architectural Review Boards) has too much control. It's becoming an impediment. 300 locations for a bank turnkey renovation – LL approval, etcetera – the processes are all becoming more and more cumbersome.

Grace: If you can wave a magic wand and change one thing in our industry – what would it be?

Jeff: OHSA – most over reaching organizations, safety regulations are essential but they take it to a level that doesn't make sense. These OHSA folks are not well trained – they are just monitoring. For example, stepping into the bucket without a harness on - even though they are still on the ground and putting it on is a $5,000.00 violation. It's become a profit center for the government. We have safety meetings every two weeks, all harnesses and safety equipment are provided, a log is kept.

Grace: What advice can you give to other business owners still growing their businesses in our industry?

Jeff: It's important to hire good people for the stuff you're not good at or don't like to do. This way you're focusing on your strengths. Also, as you grow your business, you'll find you go from trying to be all things to all people to really defining the business to what it should be. A smaller glazer company, who was having difficulty going on to the next level, recently asked me how I did it. You have to have the courage to take a big job, grow your capabilities to fit the job. If you're going to be intimated by the big job you can't handle - you'll always be small. Time after time - whether it's to buy equipment or open another office – it's all growing pains and you need courage to accept these big challenges.

Grace: Do you love what you do? How important do you feel it is for a leader – to absolutely love what they do?

Jeff: Yes, I love what I do. I grew up in it. Loving what you do is vital to your success.

Grace: What are the top 3 traits you feel make up strong Leadership?

Jeff: Lead by example is number 1. I would never ask anyone to do anything that I wouldn't, couldn't or haven't done. The way we use to hang signs back in the day was life risking! If someone calls me and says they can't do the job with over ½ M in the latest equipment –I'll tell them to punch out – wait for me to get on site and I'll show him how it's taken care of.

Secondly, treat your employees as equals, as human beings. I don't consider myself better than anyone. It's important to treat people fairly.

Third, admit or identify your shortcomings. Don't be afraid to admit it. Hire people in place to do what you can't do or if they can do it better.

Grace: What are the top 3 traits you feel make up strong Teams?

Jeff: The first is enthusiasm. The second is spirit of cooperation, teamwork. The third is humility. You want people that are aggressive and assertive with self confidence but it needs to be tempered with humility. It starts with personality, people have to be teachable – the minute you think you know it all – the day you think you know it all that's when there's trouble.

Grace: What is the most important lesson you've learned in this industry that will help someone else along their career path?

Jeff: Quality. Set a high standard of quality. I will not sacrifice quality – value engineering is important but never to the point of shabbiness. You never go sub-standard, just don't take the job. A lot of people do that and cut corners.

Grace: If you had to do it all over again – what, if anything, would you do differently?

Jeff: There's not a lot I would change because I realize a lot of things that made life difficult ultimately made you stronger in the end. ADVERSITY.

Grace: Who was the most impactful role model or mentor for you? How have they impacted your career? Your life?

Jeff: Freddy Miller from Midtown Neon. He had a work ethic that I admired but also came to realize he lived to work. I work to live. Freddy was in the office early at 7am; worked 6 or

7 days a week. He made sure everything he touched, every job that went through that place - made huge margins. He had a lot of relationships and I realized how important business relationships are. He encouraged and supported my entrepreneurship – he would sub contract work to me.

Grace: Are you a role model or mentor for someone else?

Jeff: My son, not only in the business environment – but I had to work hard to be the father to him since I was not encouraged by my father. I'm in a position to mentor him.

Grace: Finish this sentence: One word that exemplifies life is...

Jeff: One word to exemplify my life – ADVERSITY. All the things I had to overcome are by far the biggest motivating successes in both business and personal. Survival skills applied to business. The more stuff to plow through - the stronger it makes you.

About Jeff

In 1970 Jeff Petersen started working part time after school and weekends at a small local sign company. In 1972 he graduated high school, joined sheet metal local union #137 and began his official apprenticeship. For the next four years he worked at two large NYC sign companies where he honed his fabrication and installation skills. During these years he built some of the largest Times Square spectacular displays. In 1976 he completed his apprenticeship and at this time relocated, bringing his wife and 5 year old daughter to follow his parents and siblings to Hawaii. This is when his entrepreneurial juices started flowing. He would cruise Waikiki and other bustling night spots looking for broken neon or fluorescent outages, returning the next day to sell the repair job. After several months his small business started to grow. One day while at a car dealership to sell them a repair, he was offered a job selling used cars. He accepted to hone his sales skills and within 3 months he was top salesman for the next year and a half. In 1978 Jeff returned to NY where he worked through a union for a short time. In 1979 Jeff started T.J. Signs. Since then he's grown the company to over 25M in sales with facilities in three states. In 2012 the company was sold to a private equity group for 24M.

CHAPTER 6

Everything I Learned in Kindergarten Still Applies in Business Today: Be a Good Listener and Always Use Please and Thank You.

By Tracy Sinnott

A long time ago in the 80's at the very start of my career, I was trying very hard to be promoted to the next level of management. I was accepting transfers from one restaurant to another throughout the state where I currently lived as well as grew up in. One morning I received a call from my manager (it was extremely early). This manager told me in very angry nasty words to get my butt back to the restaurant ASAP to clean up the mess I had left when I closed. As I was driving to the restaurant, I wondered what could I have missed and how was I going to handle the situation with the very angry manager when I got there. When I arrived, I was greeted by an angry manager who was over the top with exaggeration on what the problem was. When she showed me the dried up spill under the filing cabinet in the manager's office I could not believe she even had the nerve to call me in much less talk to me the way she was. The spill could have been there for days and really was a minor issue. I cleaned up the spill without a word, said goodbye and left. I left with two very valuable lesson that early morning.

Lesson 1: Follow through on the boss's expectation 100%. Lesson 2: Always treat people with respect. It does not matter what the issue is everyone deserves to be treated with respect and dignity. There is a difference between having a tough conversation around accountabilities and yelling or degrading a person for their mistakes/ performance. All these years later, I do not disagree with having been called in to correct my mistake; I only disagree with how it was handled.

I am happy to say everything did work out for me and I was promoted and stayed with the company for more than nine years. During those years, I worked with many wonderful people who taught me so many things about people development, taking responsibility for your own development and the art of mentorship. Since then I have worked for many top name retailers and restaurants and I have met so many great people that have influenced me in many ways to help become the person I am today. The best part of working for these top companies and moving around the country is that I met my husband. My husband is the kindest and most patient person I have ever met. He has helped me find the strength to get up and speak to over five hundred people, he has encouraged me to take positions traveling to Europe and across the States opening new restaurants while he stays at home and works on his career and holds the fort down.

Now many years later and in a different place in my career and life, the lesson of remembering to be kind still resonates with me every day… My kids are now teenagers and being a working mom, everything I have learned in the business world works at home. The lesson sounds quite easy but you have to think about how every word, action and even your body language are perceived. Since having children, I decided to work in the world of Franchising to have more flexibility in my schedule and still learn and grow in the business world. To be a successful member of the franchising team the first step in being successful is being a good listener. I have learned that working in the franchise world it does not matter if you are speaking to an owner who has 15 units or an owner who has 100 units the job is to understand the needs of the franchisee and incorporate them into keeping with the brand standards. The only way to understand the needs of the ownership is to listen. I have included some of the steps I find to be most important; they are not in order of any importance as they all are equally important. However, they will be most effective if you incorporate all of them when working with your team.

- Always be kind, talk to the people you work with (including those you work for, your peers and subordinates) learn something about them. People love to talk about themselves especially when someone seems genuinely interested. The most important lesson here is that you have to remember what they told you. (Commit it to memory or carry 3x5 cards or a notebook, write down what you learned after you leave) The next time you see them, you should ask them about what they told you… their dog, a goal they were trying to obtain, kids, a vacation and so on. A solid trusting working relationship does not happen overnight but if you start with being a good listener and being kind to whom you are working with you will have a good start.

- Thanking people for the work they do goes a long way however it must be sincere. I remember when I was training to be a manager for a retail chain and every night when we were closed, cleaned up and ready to leave the manager would say "great job everyone, have a good night'" I would always think to myself, WOW not everyone gave a 100% tonight. Then one night the owner worked a shift with us and he was calling out specific people and thanking them for something they had done. After a while, everyone was strutting around trying to outdo each other to get a complement from the owner. I decided when I was running my own store I would look for reasons to compliment people for a specific thing they did really well. That night changed how I would manage the people forever. That means you have to look and listen for people doing a good job and make a mental note to let them know you appreciated the work they did. Do not forget about the folks not meeting your expectations, you can address them one on one and talk about what they do well but they could make it even better with a few tweaks.

- Find things to compliment people on that are important to the business. They have to be clear on the expectations. So setting the expectation is a very important step, be clear - ask the person if they understand the expectation. Always explain the "whys" of the expectation and be sure to follow up on the expectation, check in and ask questions. Reward through positive communication and added responsibilities or autonomy. Never allow silent approvals, even if it seems to be a small issue. Communication is the key in any situation and the more positive you can keep it the better the outcome. Positive communication does not mean that you cannot be fiercely honest and clear if you are disappointed with a situation or outcome.

- Be a good listener. This is a learned behavior you must practice. Sometimes being a good listener requires patience. Do not be afraid of the silence that may loom for what seems minutes. Wait for the person to gather their thoughts and when they do speak listen carefully to what they have to say. When listening do not think about your next comment, really listen and you might learn something. I always try to repeat what I think the person is saying so they know I understand them clearly. I think being a good listener is the ultimate act of kindness in the business world and it works for your everyday life as well. Think about this... have you ever been around the person who does not hear a word you're saying, they just keep spewing words talking over you. There is nothing more annoying and it is very counterproductive. I am sure anyone stuck in a conversation like this and thinking WOW I will never get those 30 minutes back! It also makes you wonder how this person really functions day in and day out not being involved in anything but himself or herself. I honestly doubt that a person can ever be successful without the skill of listening.

I have worked in restaurant and retail domestically, as well as, international and the lesson I learned in the 80's is still relevant. The keys for me being successful are clear; take the time to learn the business first. Understand the objectives and understand how the people you interact with on the day-to-day fit within the organization. Work very hard at getting to know and understand the people you will work with and learn how their goals fit with the organization. Know what motivates the individuals you work with or better yet, what really makes them tick... Once you understand the people, you then know how to best support them and what tactics will work. Communicate the expectations clearly, listen carefully, and always be kind and follow up using positive reinforcements whenever possible. Finally, yet most importantly, being successful does not only mean you are doing well in your career - it also means you have found balance, peace, and happiness in your private life. Take the time to find your happy place - the rewards are great!

About Tracy

Tracy Sinnott is an operations executive with over 30 years of experience in start-ups, turn-arounds and day-to-day operations in both company operations and franchise operations. Tracy has worked in retail and restaurant operations, starting out working for her father in his franchised business in Minnesota in the late 70's. After working for her father through school, she has worked for many wonderful people who have inspired her and led her with grace. Tracy defines her success in the workplace through collaboration with team members whether they are key operators within the organization, franchise owners, and or franchise operators to measurably improve performance in the areas of sales, traffic, strong margins, and guest experience. Tracy's greatest success to date is her marriage to her wonderful husband Steve and her two teenage children Dillon and Michaela. As a family, they like to travel, dine out, spend time with friends and family, and build lasting memories. Tracy and her family live in the suburbs of Chicago. Being successful is finding the balance to love, live healthy and prosper.

CHAPTER 7

Interview Chat

with Dean Jones

Grace: Dean, a little bit about your background first. Where did you grow up? How big was your family?

Dean: I grew up in Dickenson ND, small town 15-16,000 when I was growing up; now it's 22,000 with oil boom. Verizon doesn't have any corporate stores there – only an agent store.

Grace: Do you remember the first store you shopped at or the first restaurant you ate in?

Dean: Restaurant – I don't remember. Would've have probably been a mom and pop restaurant. The first store, a national chain, was Woolworth. It was large chain and the Walmart of its' time in our home town. As a kid you can get anything you wanted there.

Grace: What schools did you attend? How much experience did you get hands on?

Dean: Little of both – I did grow up in a construction family. My dad owned his own construction company – that did commercial construction. I went to college at North Dakota State University in Fargo. I was in a facilities management program - although it was not accredited then but part of an interior design program. I bounced between construction management, interior design and facilities.

Grace: What was your first job in this niche industry?

Dean: Facilities and Construction coordinator for the phone book company GTE directories. I was on the corporate side, based out of Dallas. It felt like I was thrown to the wolves, running big projects, but it was a good learning ground especially since the first project was renovating the President's office! Later I was sent to Chicago to run the region with the whole intent to shut down the regional quarters that time. I was only 6 months out of school when I was in that job. This was a leadership role very early on. I taught me to manage staff at an off site office.

Grace: Which was your favorite job in this niche industry?

Dean: Today's job! Verizon. It's the brand, the people, the culture of the company. It's the work I do – all facets of the business – from site selection, lease negotiations to construction and facilities management. I have a great team of 42 people reporting to me.

Grace: Having been in our industry this long, as an industry thought leader - what do you think we're doing great in this industry? What do you feel we are excelling at?

Dean: A lot of things, understanding and balancing our internal customers – their needs and expectations with the cost of business. Technology has played a pivotal role in helping with that.

Grace: With all your experiences in our brick and mortar world - what do you think we can improve upon as an industry?

Dean: We still have room to improve upon technology, our industry is slower to adapt to technology. We need to embrace sustainability initiatives in the industries. Verizon is doing more and more of that.

Grace: If you can wave a magic wand and change one thing in our industry – what would it be?

Dean: See more and more collaboration and benchmarking between retailers. I think we have some more room to grow. There are people driving it from the professional organizations and tradeshows.

Grace: Do you love what you do?

Dean: Yes!

Grace: How important do you feel it is for a leader – to absolutely love what they do?

Dean: You have to have a passion for what you do in this business. In our industry you don't have a long shelf life if you don't love what you do. I have a tremendous amount of respect and recognition for my team, for the industry. You have to have a passion for what you do.

Grace: What are the top 3 traits you feel that make up strong leadership?

Dean:

1. Integrity. In everything you do must have a high level of integrity, has to be the core of who you are.

2. Not being afraid to challenge the status quo – not about just fixing what's broke.

3. Being decisive – you must be a decision maker. I tell my team that we are all going to make mistakes, but we will learn from the mistakes we make. You can't be afraid of making mistakes, you need to be decisive.

Grace: What are the top 3 traits you feel that make up strong teams?

Dean:

1. Diverse backgrounds, each bringing different talents and experiences.

2. Flexibility

3. Trust for a bigger cause. It's not about me; it's more about the team. There's no personal glory.

Grace: What is the most important lesson you've learned in this industry that will help someone else along their career path?

Dean: The biggest thing I learned was being flexible. This is especially important early in your career to get experience, life experience. I was able to move to get a job, went to Poland, Dominican Republic to run jobs. Be open to new opportunities to broaden your experience. In Poland and Dominican Republic I was still working for GTE Directories. I was setting up new offices and hiring staff. I worked with different people from different cultures. A year and a half after college – I was doing international work. I miss it a little bit – it was challenging, fun, an adventure!

Grace: If you had to do it all over again – what, if anything, would you do differently?

Dean: I would've gotten into retail earlier in my career. I had great experiences in the corporate side – but I really love retail! My first retailer role started as a facilities manager. I have been with Verizon for over 18 years. Since October 2000 I was doing this job as Director of Real Estate.

Grace: Who was the most impactful role model or mentor for you? And how have he or she impacted your career? Your life?

Dean: My father. My father taught me strong work ethic; integrity and respect for others by watching him grow and manage his business. He retired but still doing project management; a freelance construction manager - managing multiple jobs. My brother is a general contractor, doing mechanical work in industrial plants. My mom was a stay at home mom.

Grace: Are you a role model or mentor for someone else?

Dean: I hope I am for my daughters. They are 8 and 4 years old. I hope I can do for them as my father has for me. At work, I hope I'm a mentor for my team as well.

About Dean

Dean Jones is Director of Retail Real Estate and Facilities for Verizon Wireless. He is responsible for the company's retail real estate, design, construction and facility management functions for the South Area. Dean's efforts cover 11 states, over 500 retail and 60 administrative properties equaling more than four million square feet.

Dean's experience in the wireless industry spans 18 years, all with Verizon Wireless and its predecessor companies. He has held leadership roles of increasing responsibility including, Strategic Services Manager, Facilities Management Administrator and Building Planner, to name a few.

Dean holds a Bachelor of Science degree in Interior Design, with an emphasis in Facility Management from North Dakota State University, Fargo, North Dakota.

CHAPTER 8

ALL ABOARD!

By Lisa Johnson

———————◆•◆———————

Life is an extraordinary train that you don't want to miss. It takes you through and around places; people and things that you never knew existed until you experience them for yourself. Each and every stop along the way is unique in its experience, yet also familiar. Each stop plays an amazing role in the direction our lives are headed. I am so grateful for all the events in my life. They have led me to many places and taught me how important it is to be a part of something that is bigger than me. It taught me to be part of a team. As children, we learn the fundamentals of being a part of a family. We understand that decisions we make affect each other. As leaders our choices and goals become more complex; we learn how we affect more than just our families. It's then we seek within and ask: Are we just thinking about ourselves or do we want to be a part of something bigger?

I have been involved in the sign industry for more than 21 years. Like my father, I grew up in the industry. In my current role as VP of Project Management at Interstate Signcrafters, I oversee both new and rebrand jobs. Both types of jobs have their own challenges. With rebrands there are varying site conditions that require us to be fluid with what the municipalities and landlords dictate. New jobs have more creativity and diversity but also require learning and understanding of the different personalities.

Throughout my career, I have worked hard to overcome the stigma of being the boss's daughter. I've learned the business from the ground up. Being in the trenches with the team – I've fought hard and earned the respect and approachability from my team members. I am hard on myself, but this creates an internal drive in me. I've also been fortunate to have a mentor: Lisa Cappiello. Lisa Cappiello was the office manager at American Signcrafters, when I worked at the NY Facility. She was great at it because she could be real with people and that allowed people to be real with her. She always knew the right questions to ask: "How can we fix this? How can we make this better?" I trained and learned so much under Lisa. I learned to read people better and understand where they were coming from. I learned to dig down to the root of any concerns or challenges they had as well as understand their intentions. Maintaining a positive relationship with my team members – I also notice the subtleties of what keeps them peppy. Team and field team members know when leaders invest into this relationship and they drive and thrive on that.

As a leader, I've learned to recognize employees and also get the employees involved. There are times when we vote on "Who was most inspiring and why?" Then I'll take everyone's feedback and share with the team - this is what your coworkers think about you and why. Some are serious, some are funny with nicknames – but they're all always motivating. At safety breakfast meetings –we tie in personal associate announcements as well: birthdays, new babies or grand babies. We keep people informed on what's going on behind the scenes so they can get inspired on what's coming on the horizon and recognize there's more room for them to grow. The communication with my team is the big differentiator because most other companies don't take the time to do this. This builds bonds and creates a company culture.

A couple of years back our professional team grew very quickly. Growth in anything, whether it be personally or in business, can either be distracting or so inspiring it makes you strive to be a better person. I was so inspired by what I saw take place around me and so grateful to work with so many incredible people, that it only made me want to do more. I believe it had that same effect on the rest of the team. We had work coming out of our ears, but never had a happier workforce that I recall in the history of the company. People worked so hard their entire bodies ached, but the smile never left their faces. Management and employees alike, worked side by side to meet the deadlines of such demanding timelines, and never lost their sense of humor. Everyone had such a desire to succeed together as one unit. We invested in each other and picked each other up when things became difficult. Not to be cliché, but it was the "all for one and one for all" mentality. Not one person was on their own little island. People's families pulled together and pitched in when kids needed to be cared for after school. Some wives would stop in with freshly baked goods to distribute on break. Others would make home cooked meals, enough for everyone to eat instead of eating fast food or sandwiches. In walking the floor, people would tell me they never wanted to work so hard for a company as much as they did here because the atmosphere was so amazing; people cared about so much more than just themselves. Everyone pulled together to make sure we stayed on track and committed to seeing it through. It was grueling at times but rewarding to see the accomplishments of many. People grew so much and learned how to be a part of something bigger than themselves.

We've had a lot of the same people that have worked here throughout the years, some as long as 19 years. Associates who have left and come back always say "Ah I'm home." All throughout, the culture never really changed because we were always on track with the right culture. So what's the ingredient to a successful culture? What makes people invest and make sacrifices to see everyone gain success? Some people would say its money, and let's face it, that's a definite motivator. But this scenario was much more than that. There was camaraderie. There was leadership and team work.

Leadership. Be genuine. People need to see you are a real person. You're here to do business but also you are not selling them a bill of goods, you're going to back the team. You need a strong presence but that does not mean you're walking around with a big stick. You set boundaries. Be approachable. Approachability is necessary. If your team can't approach you they will not have your back – they will be afraid. It is a mutual partnership. People buy into who you are as a leader, who you are as person – the direction of the company. We've shed blood, sweat and tears – literally at times, to get to the next level as a company.

Team. First everyone needs to realize that in a team – it's not about the individual. You're not trying to stand out, be on your own island or use someone else's back as a platform to excel. When you come together as a team everyone has a common goal, a group direction. Everyone wants to be recognized but it's about the team first. There is strength in recognizing each other's talents. Everyone's combined strengths create a winning team. If people can just take a step back and examine what each individual has to offer, this is what you have to offer, this is what I have to offer and this is how we can work together to make this fly. Because team members remain teachable, they absorb so much more from their team mates that they will propel each other out of the box and promote creativity.

I don't have all the answers but I do know one thing. A commitment to being a part of something bigger than ourselves is critical to success. When that extraordinary train of life approaches the station, remember- you can effectively make this choice. When those doors open, I hope everyone chooses to step aboard, onto something greater and commit to being a part of a team all travelling to the same destination.

ABOUT LISA

Lisa Johnson is the Vice President of Interstate Signcrafters. Her focus has been on managing both the Project Management and Sales Teams. Her career in the sign industry started at American Signcrafters in New York, 21 years ago. Lisa started by answering phones in the reception area, to assisting sales associates and senior PM's, then on to learning everything from inception to completion with various different projects, both on local and national levels. Since then, the company expanded to South Florida in 1997, where Lisa has been managing teams in their 40,000 square foot facility in Boynton Beach for the past fifteen years. Ultimately a team was built alongside her, where she would teach, mentor, motivate, build relationships, create and problem solve with many talented people.

Lisa has fostered long term business relationships with her clients that span decades. She is well known for her professionalism, on time and in budget delivery with just the right touch of humor and laughter that helps ease all stressful situations her clients are under.

When not assisting clients with their signage needs, Lisa enjoys spending time with her husband of 9 years, Bryan and their 4 month old daughter, Rebecca. Lisa currently resides in Lake Worth, Florida with her family.

CHAPTER 9

Interview Chat

with Tim Anderson

Grace: Let's start with some background. Where did you grow up, Tim?

Tim: I grew up in New Haven, Connecticut. I'm the youngest of 4 kids; I have 2 brothers and a sister.

Grace: Do you remember the first store you shopped at or the first restaurant you ate in?

Tim: Alexander's for back to school shopping. I remember McDonald's – it was old school! It had just golden arches and you eat in your car!

Grace: What schools did you attend?

Tim: St. Francis of Assisi in Fair Haven, Connecticut grammar school. Eli Whitney High School.

Grace: What was your first job in this niche industry?

Tim: SS Kresge store in downtown New Haven, Connecticut. I worked there during high school, after school.

Grace: Which was your favorite job in this niche industry?

Tim: I enjoyed every job. Every level gave me knowledge for the future. I was fortunate to work with characters, fun people, smart people who knew their positions inside and out... and some not so sharp on their scope of work. Made it clear to me my family was right: Whatever you do – do it well! Be the best at it!

Grace: As an industry thought leader, what do you think we're doing great in this industry? What are we excelling at?

Tim: We are thinking out of the box. Trying new things in the design of our stores, making the experience happen at every sense... Smell, touch, sound!!

Grace: What do you think we can improve upon as an industry?

Tim: Relationships. There's got to be a connection to your vendor – especially your GC.

Grace: If you can wave a magic wand and change one thing in our industry – what would it be?

Tim: Just make it happen. There are too many people who focus on what they can't do instead of what they can do.

Grace: Do you love what you do?

Tim: YES, ABSOLUTELY!!

Grace: How important do you feel it is for a leader – to absolutely love what they do?

Tim: When you're passionate about your job it's contagious. If a leader doesn't love what they do everything comes across flat. Why bother then? There's no excitement, no movement forward!

Grace: What are the top 3 traits you feel make up strong Leadership?

Tim: Communication. Passion. Positive at at all times!! Not just when it's easy!

Grace: What are the top 3 traits you feel make up strong Teams?

Tim: 1. Diversity in what each team member brings to the table. 2. Clear division of responsibilities from the Team Leader. 3. Communication.

Grace: What is the most important lesson you've learned in this industry that will help someone else along their career path?

Tim: Be true to yourself and your beliefs. If you find yourself somewhere that fundamentally challenges your core beliefs – make a change – that's not home! Always know that everyone has something to offer – from the most entry level person to the most senior. Be open to learn no matter what your age or level. Also, be open to share your knowledge!

Grace: If you had to do it all over again – what, if anything, would you do differently?

Tim: NOTHING! Life is what you make of it. I live life fully and have NO REGRETS!!

Grace: Who was the most impactful role model or mentor for you? How have they impacted your career and ultimately your life?

Tim: There's been a few along the way. As surprised as people are when I say some of the worse bosses had the biggest impact. They teach us what not to do…how it feels first hand to be handled in a negative manner – and how you say in your head I will NEVER do that to anyone! I was brought up in a family that "no" wasn't an option, that we could achieve whatever we wanted as long as we worked hard. My earlier role models were strong willed, hard working people. Along the way in business and in life, I believe you pick up things along the way from everyone you meet. It creates the person you are. Don't underestimate the power of one…and the power – even a quick conversation can change the life of someone. You being in the right place at the right time.

Grace: Are you a role model or mentor for someone else?

Tim: I certainly hope so. I try to be. I'm a mentor that teaches by example. One of my favorite quotes is "go forth and teach… and if you must – use words!" I think a gentle guide is always the most important way to assist…but hey, I work a lot in New York City so sometimes a big shove is needed – and I can do that as well!

Grace: Please provide one word that best describes this industry and then explain why you've chosen that word.

Tim: Change… One of my first mentors told me the only thing constant in retail is nothing is constant. You need to always evolve! Never think you have arrived or you know the answer. Appreciate that your customer changes, evolves and so must you.

Grace: What are you most grateful for in this industry?

Tim: The fun!!! Keeping up with the change... Striving for perfection...Wanting to give the very best experience to your customer is a rush! It keeps me connected, curious and resourceful!

Grace: Where do you find your inspiration?

Tim: Everywhere... Anywhere... You need to keep your mind totally open. Not easy but if you can - do it. You'll see inspiration in the most unusual places!! I'm constantly taking pictures. Running up and feeling something to see if the touch equals the vision. I love New York City...the restaurants, the architecture, the markets, the parks, the museums and even the subway! You can find inspiration sitting on a bench in Union Square as the world strolls by!

About Tim

Tim Anderson is the Vice President of Store Design and Construction for Aeropostale, Inc. Aeropostale, Inc. is a mall-based, specialty retailer of casual apparel and accessories, principally targeting 14 to 17 year-old young women and men through its Aéropostale® stores and 4 to 12 year-old children through its P.S. from Aéropostale® stores. Tim leads a team that handles all of the design for stores in their International markets as well as the Store Design and Construction for all stores in North America.

Tim has over 25 Years of experience in retail. He has held various positions with several leading retailers, starting in Operations as a Store Manager and District Manager and then moving into Store Development. When not involved in the many aspects of his life, Tim resides in West Haven, CT with his two grown children. His passions include traveling the world and volunteering.

CHAPTER 10

Speeding Along the Subway

By Michael Fairclough

———————◆•◆•◆———————

According to the classical model of physics, there is nothing new in the universe. All of the constituents of the atoms that make up our world have been here since the beginning, whenever that was. So, the idea of creating something new is theoretically impossible; we simply rearrange what was already there. Therein lies one of the most valuable lessons I've ever learned: It's all about perspective. The scientific giants of history explored the natural world around them and provided the people with an understanding, a new perspective on the way things are. Great modern thinkers from Picasso to Steve Jobs have stretched the boundaries by exploring new ways of looking at things. The pursuit of new ideas, new frontiers and a new mindset built on the collective learning of our history is a fundamental human experience, and it has shaped who we are today.

There's a way to do it better—find it. -Thomas Edison

One of the most difficult things for me to do is to consider that the current way I am going about things might need to change; still, I believe I understand Edison here. I feel that he was aware that human history had continually proven itself to be in a constant state of change, a forward movement toward development and discovery. His quote is less a challenge and more a conviction, a resignation to the state of things and a call to arms to embrace the notion of change; it can be argued that it is practically un-human to not do so. I hope to introduce two very different stories, both of which explore the impact of a small change in approach which, as a result, revealed an entirely new understanding of human nature.

The Subway

I love New York City. The sheer scale of the city humbles me. When I'm there, I feel a strong sense of opportunity mixed with a comfortable sense of anonymity. I do my best to blend in and explore while I'm there, and I've never been disappointed. When I was a kid, I read a book called *Slakes Limbo*, a story about a boy who ran away from home and lived in the subway system. He earned money by picking up discarded newspapers and then selling them to waiting passengers. He lived in the tunnels, slept on a discarded mattress, dipped sugar cubes in his coffee, people-watched, helped those who were lost, and had created his own identity in the dark and musky filth of a subway—and I loved it. I myself constantly rode the subway in New York. Over time I began to get around the city rather easily and found myself more than willing to offer tourists directions and routes to get to where they wanted to go, just like Slake. However, there is another story here.

New York City is anything but simple, and its subway is no different. There are 430 stops and over 3 million riders each day speaking over 120 languages, from Ph.D.'s to GED's to children, all relying on the system for transportation. In 1972, the Metropolitan Transportation Authority reached out to a world-renowned graphic designer with a challenge to develop a guide that made sense of the complexity of the subway system. The MTA's guide, prior to 1972, had evolved quite a bit as new tracks and lines were implemented, and the MTA felt that the visual element needed some strategic design to help its riders.

The response to the challenge was, in my opinion, the most beautifully designed representation of the subway ever. The designer color-coded lines, represented all stops by a simple dot, and streamlined the flow of the tracks by representing them as vertical, horizontal, or 45-degree planes. It is a rather comforting and approachable guide to use, and certainly aligned its content with the cognitive abilities of the varied population that would actually use it.

By the mid-to-late-1970s, this new guide was no longer used, and a new designer was hired. What happened?

The guide answered the wrong challenge. The new guide, albeit beautiful, legible, and clear, ended up actually confusing and distorting the reality of NYC. In effort to implement the minimalist principles to the new visual guide, the designer distorted the physical geography of the city. In fact, Central Park is represented as a square, when all New Yorkers know that it's a rectangle. A rider would read the guide and exit at 81st Street at the Natural Museum thinking it was a short walk to the north border of Central Park, when in fact it's more than a mile. In the designer's defense, he really wasn't attempting to make a map at all; in fact, he never called it a map. It seems as if the designer was seeking to answer the question: "How do I navigate the subway system most efficiently?" and in those terms I feel he accomplished his goal. However, that question wasn't on the minds of the subway users. The subway users wanted to know: "How do I get to my destination?" and as far as I know, only Slake lived in the subway system. Everyone else lived and worked on the streets above the subway.

Here's a thought to consider: When efficiency trumps effectiveness, it is no longer efficient.

So, while the 1972 map did achieve a level of simplicity that had never been previously achieved, it actually got people lost. The MTA went back to the designer with their feedback but the designer stood his ground, defending that his design accomplished its goal. Later, the MTA hired a designer named Hertz who created the subway map that is in current use. This current map implemented many of the successful design components used in the 1972 guide and added to it a scalable geography, and was supplemented by station-specific maps displaying the surrounding area at street-level detail. Hertz understood that the map had to be effective and that a level of complexity was necessary to get people wherever they were try to go. Still, I'm fairly certain that without the 1972 guide, the current MTA map would not have lasted so long. Who knows what the future holds for the MTA subway map, but I'm sure that there is a better way, and even more certain that someone will find it.

Speeding Alfa Romeos

It seems logical that a speeding ticket should be a sufficient deterrent to prevent hazardous driving. In Italy, the city government felt that it would be worthwhile to post a live radar reading alongside a long stretch of country road. When the driver would pass by, an actual speed reading was displayed right next to the posted speed limit. The idea was to appeal to the logic of the speeder. If a driver was speeding and saw that his speed was being tracked, the most logical thing to do would be to slow down and avoid the risk of a ticket. As it turned out, this was not as effective as the city had hoped; the net reduction in speeding was very low. The goal was simple: Keep the roads safe. Here, however, common sense wasn't working, and the city had to use some uncommon sense.

The city recognized that people were in fact reading the display, but the display didn't trigger a response to slow down. A crazy idea was brought to the table for discussion on the problem and proved too far more effective at road safety than the city had hoped.

What was it? The city kept the speed reading but added a happy or sad face below it, depending on whether the driver was within the limit (happy face) or speeding (sad face). Remarkably, the emotional connection these faces made was enough to trigger the tap on the brakes the city was aiming for.

The lesson is unmistakable: The effective choice is often not the most logical, but the most insightful.

About Michael

Michael Fairclough is the Executive Vice President of Resicom, having joined the company in 1997. Michael grew up in Chicago and its' surrounding suburbs. He currently lives in Carlsbad CA with his wife and two sons.

During the week, you can find him in his office at 8am with a Peet's coffee and a desk full of water bottles. His daily focus is dedicated to raising the level of awareness of the importance of atmospherics and the role it plays in driving retail brands to success. An avid entrepreneur, Michael left Chicago to spearhead the development of Resicom's west coast growth initiative. Starting from a satellite office in his home, Michael developed an office and team of over 25 full time employees simply through the application of Resicom's core values. A new practitioner of yoga and a mountain biking enthusiast, Michael loves the access to the outdoors and active lifestyle that California brings.

CHAPTER 11

Developing Your Own Leadership Style from a Late Bloomer

By Jon Baumann

H ow does this come about? Is it conscious or subconscious in nature? For me, it was almost by accident. Coming from a large family (pretty common in the Midwest), I was the 10th of 11 children. This simply meant that I got what the others were finished with (clothes, toys, etc.). However, I didn't lack any attention from either of my parents, who remained happily married until they passed on. If you can imagine 8 boys and 3 girls over the span of 15 years—quite an intimate setting, to say the least, but we had an outstanding wiffle ball team without needing to include any of the neighbors. With very little resources, our parents were able to put all of us through Christian day school—not an easy task given the number of mouths to feed.

I started my working career at the age of 15 years old delivering newspapers for a local news agency. It was an expectation that as soon as you were able to work, you were doing so to help with the bills. As my high school years rolled on, I left the newspaper business and got a part-time job bagging groceries at a local grocery store through the school distributive education program. This is when it really began.

Once high school was over, an opportunity came along to work full-time overnight at a different grocery chain. I jumped at the opportunity to try to generate some cash and benefits. You see, with a house full of siblings and a father who was working two jobs to make ends meet, college just wasn't on the radar for most of my siblings. Without any real future plans, I worked the overnights for quite a few years until I was asked to take on a position of more responsibility, because apparently my work ethic and consistency were recognized by those making the decisions. After running the overnight crews for several years, an opportunity came along to move back to the day shift as a manager. Shocked that I would even be considered, I was thrilled to move up the food chain and contribute at a higher level (let alone a pay increase).

This is where I ran into a gentleman named Bob—unbeknownst to me at the time, my very first real mentor. Bob had great confidence in my abilities, even when I wasn't sure myself. Over the course of the next three years, he promoted me three times until I got the opportunity to run my very own store. Bob used to say to me, "What are you afraid of? What's the worst thing that could happen?" It was at that point that I really started to gain confidence in my abilities. I was moved to several other locations as manager and thought I had achieved everything that I possibly could.

One day, I received a call from a new retailer that was going to be opening a store in my neighborhood. They wanted me to come by for an interview to manage this location. The doubt began to return as I wondered if I was going to get in over my head by going somewhere unfamiliar. Just the same, I went for the interview to see what this was all about—mostly curiosity, I guess.

I was quite nervous and unsure of myself, mostly because there were a lot of other candidates there and most were very seasoned veterans. Surely they stood a better chance than I. Just the same, my opportunity came to be interviewed for the very first time. I had no idea what I was supposed to ask or say, and frankly was sweating bullets, wondering why I had made the decision to do this. I started feeling disloyal to the company I was currently working for after all they had done for me.

As the questioning began, I was pleasantly surprised. The questions were very basic in nature, and most of them were common sense to answer. "As a manager, how can you tell when you have dissention within your employees?" Pretty simple to me: "I just eavesdrop on their conversations from the next aisle over." The interviewer started laughing. "That is probably the best response I have ever had to that question," he said. My concerns of inadequacy were now gone, and I sailed through the interview and got the job. You see, apparently naive honesty was refreshing to this gentleman, compared to the hard-to-believe stories he usually heard during interviews.

Satisfied with this turn of events, I worked at this job for the next 10 years, during which I was asked to help open many new stores, hire employees, and other duties. Then I got the call... It was the corporate office calling: "We're going to be opening a couple of hundred stores, and we want you to come to the corporate office to assist in the process." You see, though I wasn't aware of it at the time, I had the only real working copies of "the process." Over time, I had accumulated a portfolio of miscellaneous data that was now in demand. This would require relocating myself and my family away from the only place where we had ever lived. Now, that constituted a "real" risk—the biggest risk I had ever taken in my career at that point.

After much consideration, we agreed to make the move. To say that this was stressful would be an understatement. It was a new place with new people and new responsibilities. All of that being said, I was so busy from the minute I stepped foot in my new office that I didn't have time to look back. This is when I met another mentor, Ed. Ed was tough on the outside, full of wisdom and experience, and looking for his next candidate: me!

Over the next seven years (right up until now, as a matter of fact), I have been privileged to work for this man. His ability to look inside a person and find out what makes that person tick is amazing. He moved me into a high-level position with a great deal of responsibility and turned me loose. His famous line, "You'll figure it out," still rings in my head. "I called the last three managers you worked for and some of your peers, and every one of them agreed you were the right person for the job," he said. For the first time, I really felt confident in my own abilities and hit the ground running. It appears that all of that time when I was molding and shaping my career, I had become well-rounded in many areas of responsibility. These things that I was now so good at had finally matured before my eyes.

This is the moment when the light went on and I realized that I had a lot to share, and there were many folks that were willing to listen. It was an almost "by accident" career, supported by people who saw something in me that I couldn't see. It has now become a full-blown mission of mine to share what I have learned with aspiring individuals who have something they don't even recognize: a strong work ethic, commitment and unabashed honesty.

Sometimes I think back and wonder what might have happened if I had forced my will on people and tried to step over them to get the prize. Then I go right back to my upbringing, which to this day keeps me grounded. "Stay true to yourself, and share what you know with anyone who will listen." "Invest in people, and you won't be disappointed." You don't have to be decorated with certificates of accomplishments to be recognized. You just need to be you—willing to talk about what you have been through and the lessons you have learned. I can't begin to count the number of people whose careers I have affected, but I can tell you that every time we meet, they are quick to shake my hand and say thanks. That, for me, is the ultimate prize!

About Jon

Jon Baumann is the Senior Director of Construction for Office Depot Inc. His current responsibilities include overseeing the entire Construction Department, Capital Expenditures, New Construction, Store Fixtures, Store Planning and Store Remodels. Jon has been in the industry since 1977 with experience in every functional area of both small and large boxes. He currently resides in Florida with his wife Sheila and their children Jillian & Craig.

CHAPTER 12

Interview Chat

with Bill Hoffmann

───────◆·◆·◆───────

Grace: Bill, let's start with your background. Where did you grow up?

Bill: I grew up in the south, went to high school in Florida where we caught alligators there!

Grace: How big was your family growing up?

Bill: I have two sisters, each living in Memphis and Mississippi. My folks live in North Carolina.

Grace: Do you remember the first store you shopped at or first restaurant you ate in?

Bill: As a kid, around five years old, I remember shopping at Maas Brothers department stores. There were five and dimes stores. Woolworths was huge. I remember the money trolleys in department stores.

Grace: Tell me about your schooling.

Bill: I went to college for biology and was heading to veterinary school. During high school and college I worked in construction. Along the line I stopped going to pre-vet school and started focusing more on construction.

Grace: What was your first job in this industry?

Bill: I was a laborer / carpenter – doing house building while in high school and college.

Grace: Now in our industry - what are some challenges you feel general contractors are facing?

Bill: The extremely fast paced changes. Retail constantly changes, it's so dynamic. Even the infrastructure is so dynamic – most of the time you can't get a consistent prototype. The customers want the product – but the store wants to show it off – so every store is not prototypical. A change order process example can be as follows: incandescent to florescent to LED in just lighting alone. You can totally evolve in every year relative to design. The architect is challenged to do the plans quicker. However, even with CADD, they generally do not check the engineering against the architectural plans. You're bidding what you see – but you know it may not be what the customer wants for the end product. This leads to many items missed on the drawings, which leads to more change orders that lead to an unhappy client.

Grace: Is there a way to help this process?

Bill: To help the process – negotiation may be better than bidding. But corporate America drives bidding. There will still be change orders because there is no time for architects to perform due diligence. Bottom line is driven by speed and speed causes errors and mistakes. There is no time for checks and balance. Back in the day when there were light tables and you did onion skin drawings, you'd layer the plans to achieve a check and balance. There was more time dedicated to do checks and balances. Today CADD offers the same option turning on all layers but time usually does not allow for this process. This is more prevalent with large projects than smaller projects. A lot of the smaller retailers are cookie cutter and rollout seamlessly. This is an industry driven by high end branded products, larger and vendor brand name retailers are constantly changing.

General contractors can build a shop – but may not necessarily want to design a shop. To suggest a fix on a vendor shop – there may be a lot of ego involved; people would get offended. Designers are "king" in the retail industry.

A hierarchy exists in the retail world. Designers draw the pretty pictures, architects and engineers do the plans for permitting to build the project. Option 1 is a CM manages the job, or option 2, The GC is responsible for management as well as cost control. D.F. Pray operates both as a CM or GC. Most CMs will still hide behind bad plans - if it is not on the drawings they will miss it. The GC would always fill in the gaps. Because of time constraints there are rarely perfect drawings and that's why you have drops/holes between the trades on who owns what.

Grace: What do you think we can improve upon as an industry? If you can wave a magic wand and change one thing in our industry – what would it be?

Bill: The bidding process – ensuring to compare apples to apples, oranges to oranges.

Even in the bidding process – there are exclusions. You exclude questionable and marginal items to get to the table to sit in front of the owner with the low numbers. You're putting the responsibility back on the owner to ensure there are no holes or gaps between trades. It's typical to get only two weeks to bid a large box project such as a department store remodel. Getting three weeks to bid is incredible. The challenge is as you're bidding it – there are changes that are coming during the bidding process. The owners are making changes as they go along. It might be better lighting, or what a designer wants/desires, these are owner driven changes. Even if they are surveying the space – you can't get into the walls because you're not going to do a destructive survey to catch everything behind the walls. They may not have time to do a thorough survey. Reverse auction is another process. This is usually what happens with corporate boardroom politics. Reverse auctions may give the client the best prices – but the question remains: are they going to get the change orders? It all comes down to time. The architect has to use that time to check all the drawings against each other. Make sure there are no architectural errors or conflicts in the drawings.

Grace: Bill you obviously love what you do, you're very passionate for your industry.

Bill: Yes! I maybe one of the few left! There's nothing better than finishing the product, opening the store ahead of schedule and having an elated owner or client!

Grace: What makes a project good, what's the ideal project?

Bill: Several areas to measure. 1. It's ahead of schedule or even better the job opens early. This is planned in advance. 2. Bids are under budget and *even with change orders* maintains an under budget status as long as change orders are legitimate and obvious - no reaching. 3. The contractor goes above and beyond to maintain schedule and budget by working with architects, engineers and subcontractors to achieve schedule and budgetary issues. There's no whining! Retail in itself is demanding enough without psychology and sociology to deal with. 4. A smooth process with very little owner intervention equals a great contractor!

Grace: Now conversely, what makes a project bad?

Bill: 1. It's behind schedule, it won't make the scheduled opening. Or worse, Contractor cannot or will not commit to a date. 2. It's over budget and The Contractor cannot pinpoint actual costs or overruns. This is a due to poor paperwork and back-up. 3. Change orders are "out of control". Every screw or nail not shown, is a change order. There is constant owner involvement required throughout project. 4. Construction quality is totally unacceptable. This along with, and in combination of other negative issues equates the end of the owner/contractor relationship!

Grace: In our industry, teamwork is so vital. What are the top 3 traits you feel make up strong teams?

Bill: First and foremost every team member has to be knowledgeable of their product, of their service. They have to know what they're doing in this business; they have to possess a confident knowledge of construction. Secondly, have an excellent sub contractor base. And lastly, it's the owner interaction piece and understanding how to communicate and manage their expectations with the Contractor.

Grace: What is the most important lesson you've learned in this industry that will help someone else along their career path?

Bill: Don't burn any bridges in this industry – it is so small that you will come across that person again. New York City is the smallest big city I have ever worked in before. The retail construction industry is so small here – you will always come across the same people.

Grace: Who was the most impactful role model or mentor for you? How have they impacted your career and ultimately your life?

Bill: Don Clifford at Filenes. He passed away in the early 80s. His knowledge of the business was extensive and he had an incredible patience in mentoring others. He had much more patience than me. I was in awe of him and how he kept his cool and calm. Actually he was more of my hero than a mentor. The intensity in this business comes from making that schedule. This business is almost like being on a battlefield – you never know when you're going to get "shell shocked, wounded or killed". You learn this business in the trenches and there is little option for mistakes, you either sink or swim.

Grace: Describe this industry in ONE word.

Bill: Intense. Very intense. It's also because I'm so passionate about my job. There are people that will never experience this type of intensity because they are not passionate; they are mediocre in their approach.

Grace: Bill, please finish this sentence: In this industry, I am most inspired by...

Bill: The design. In this industry the design is constantly being updated to compliment the products and the challenge is to stay on top of the latest design to maintain the competitive edge.

About Bill

Bill Hoffmann has more than 30 years of professional construction experience in design/build, ground up projects, including an extensive background in commercial construction, remodeling and project budgeting. Currently as a Director with D.F. Pray General Contractors, his areas of expertise also include aspects of sales, proposal development, estimating, staff and budget management, vendor selection and risk management. An experienced team leader, Bill works effectively providing guidance to project managers and superintendents in all departments; whether working individually or as part of a multidisciplinary team resulting in financial accountability, project controls, marketing, building strong vendor relations, risk management and timely responsiveness to client needs.

Bill fosters successful business relationships with his clients, architects and engineers by overseeing plan review through the final project completion - he remains involved throughout the life of the project. He utilizes his extensive skills, experience and training to successfully meet the needs of a diverse clientele on complex projects. His clients include Anne Klein, Filene's, JC Penney, Jones Apparel, Levis' Stores, Lord & Taylor, Macys, Nine West and Saks Fifth Avenue.

When not on a construction site, Bill enjoys hunting, fishing and horseback riding. He currently resides in Cape Cod, Massachusetts with his family.

CHAPTER 13

Parental Guidance Appreciated

By Frank J. Cupo

---◆·◆·◆---

In 1944, my father was serving on a Navy ship during World War II. His brother-in-law was serving on another ship in the same fleet. The warships were traveling in a long, straight line to their next destination. My father's brother-in-law wanted to join my dad on his ship. So, knowing that my father could talk to anyone, he approached my dad during a temporary docking. My dad made it his business to win over the commanding officer of the other ship and was successfully able to talk his brother-in-law on to his ship. The procession of crafts continued on their journey at sea. They split up, and half of the Navy vessels went in one direction, the other half in the other direction. Two days later, his brother-in-law's former boat was attacked and destroyed; there were no survivors. My dad's networking had actually saved his brother-in-law's life. Even at the young age of 19, he was able to hone a skill he would use in business for decades: personal connection. If there was someone who had the power to help people out, one way or another, my father would not only get to know him, but would make him his friend. My father was a masterful networker before the word "networking" existed. As it seems to be with all war veterans, my father never told this story, and I only found out about it at the very end of his life. As a matter of fact, I was already running my own business for many years when I learned of this amazing account, and it crystallized something about my dad that was quite evident: He was simply one of the best salesmen I had ever known.

The ultimate compliment to my dad's salesmanship was my mom's work ethic. She grew up in a broken home at a time when homes were rarely broken. Her mom was left to work around the clock for the family, and as soon as my mom was old enough, she followed suit. She was a child of the Great Depression and had no choice but to develop an ironclad work ethic. During the week, she came home from high school and every day went straight to work at my grandmother's candy store. The weekends were no different, with the majority of her time devoted to serving customers. Simply put, my mom has to be the hardest-working person I have ever known. Additionally, she was lucky enough to learn business skills in an office job at a young age—skills which gave her knowledge that many first-generation children of immigrants didn't have at the time: payroll, taxes and accounting.

The war ended, America celebrated, and my parents got married. In 1950, my grandfather ran a small textile company with a partner, but he wasn't really a salesman and he wasn't really a bookkeeper. My grandfather's luck wasn't helped by his then-partner leaving and taking whatever clients they had with him. My parents' work skills complemented each other very well, and they were the perfect new partners for my grandfather. They joined him in 1951 and began to learn the textile business. The company they formed would become Pioneer Textiles, Inc. My grandfather, having more of the technical and mechanical knowledge, operated the textile machines. My mom was in charge of supporting those machines and all payroll and bookkeeping. My dad put on his suit, gathered samples of their work (which

consisted of making children's clothes), and headed into New York City. There on a daily basis, with no formal training in business or sales, my father knocked on the door of every textile manufacturer in the city. He talked his way into meetings and convinced the heads of garment companies that the order they needed to place was with him. By 1953, my grandfather moved on, leaving this newly formed company in the hands of my mom and dad. Within the few short years they had been operating, they managed to bring in, manage and expand major textile clients in New York City, North Carolina, and Mississippi. My parents were still in their 20s and certainly had their hands full. My brother was a newborn, and they had never managed employees, let alone an entire company. The demands from their new clients were fierce, requiring my parents' operation to supply upwards of 300 dozen garments in a five-day turnaround period on completely manual machines. My mom always maintained a closely watched, perfectionist view of the company product. In addition to quality control, she interviewed and trained new employees, and maintained and developed client relations from an operational standpoint. It was my mom's job to make sure that the garments the staff had boxed as their company product were the best they could be. A perfect example of the pressure that my mom was under in terms of quality came when she discovered that the staff had boxed hundreds of dozens of garments in the wrong order. Upon hearing this from one of her biggest clients, my mom knew that the line of last resort had to fall upon her. She worked around the clock for the next two days and personally examined 2,000 dozen garments before they were shipped to that concerned client.

By the 1960s, my parents had built a staff of over 20 employees, which included garment designers, machinists, prep workers, and delivery workers. In that same period of time, they bought the building they were in, expanded it and purchased additional land adjacent to that building. As the years rolled on, their staff changed and the times changed, but one thing remained consistent: All of my parents' clients still remained. They managed to keep three of their biggest clients for over 25 years, something almost unheard of in today's business world. The 1970s came, and so did I. I still have vivid memories of driving my small red car in and out of all the large, cast-iron machines which ran day in and day out. My parents' industrial building is the place where I spent much of my childhood growing up. I helped my mom, I talked to the employees, and at one time, I even got the idea of opening my own garment store. At the ripe old age of 8 years old, I took all of the extra remnants that were left over every week, laid them out on a table, put a price tag on them, and made up a sign. I convinced every uncle and aunt I had that they just "had to buy one of these rags because it would look so much better than the clothes they were wearing."

Old-fashioned lessons in business are timeless. That is the most valuable lesson I ever learned from both my parents' being entrepreneurs. In our day and age of ultra-fast technology, impersonal and antiseptic means of communication, and dismissive so-called "customer service," basic and dedicated human connections never

die. The lessons that I still learn from listening to my mom talk about her days of running my parents' company stand in stark contrast to what, at times, surrounds me in modern business. The values that the World War II generation brought to their personal lives were also brought to their new businesses. Values so easily forgotten in today's world—sacrifice, simple honesty, and most of all, humility toward the customers and clients—were then, and continue to be today, the foundation of any new business. I recently asked my mom to name the three biggest things that she delivered to her clients. She answered: quality of products and services, meeting deadlines, and building close relationships with each individual client. What I witnessed for myself all these years, however, was the humility in which she approached every client, regardless of their size. That humility is defined as never thinking you are doing a client a favor by working for them and never forgetting that they are the lifeblood of your company.

I can only aspire to carry on the tradition of simple honesty and dedication to clients in the same manner that I observed for so many years. My mom and dad did so many things for me over the years that I really couldn't even begin to list them all, though certain things and certain moments really stand out. When it comes to business, two moments with my parents never left me. When I was trying to make a final decision about what type of company to open, I went to my dad one night. As he sat in his lounge chair reading a paper, seemingly engrossed in its subject matter, I went into my "pitch" about trying to revitalize the textile company of my parents' younger years. My dad didn't even have to think about the fact that the textile business was long gone and the reality that it was the wrong move brought on by my "family nostalgia." Without even hesitating, he picked his head up from the page, looked at me and said, "Do what you know best, and that is the property and construction business. Textiles are over in our country." Those words never left me, and the more I thought about them, the more I realized their wisdom. My dad focused me with one sentence, and I never looked back. I was already in the property management and construction business, and now I began to formulate my plan for the future.

The second "business moment" that my parents gave me was from my mom. I had woken up the first morning after quitting my corporate property job, and was about to embark on running my relatively new company full-time with no safety net.

I looked around and realized that I had walked away from a good position, with a good company and a boss whom I genuinely liked. My first reaction was: "What in the world did I just do?" My mom, whom I could always talk to, got on the phone with me and immediately grounded me. She said, "You have been working toward this for quite a while. You have clients, and you know what to do. If something goes wrong, you have your degrees and experience to fall back on; you'll get another job. This is one of those times when you have to take a chance." She helped me so much—there was no one else in my life that could have grounded me more than my mom at that moment. I never forgot her words. They sustained me when I questioned my decision.

The company I went on to form could only bear one name: Pioneer. I might not have carried on the same business my parents founded, but to honor them, I had to carry on the name. It was completely natural, and when I said it out loud, it just rolled off my tongue: "Pioneer Properties."

My dad passed away in 2006, and I can barely go an hour without thinking about him. In the last days of his life, I slept in the same room with him, which was the bedroom where I grew up. Just to be sure that I would properly carry on his life and legacy, I asked him to tell the story of how he talked his brother-in-law off of a Navy ship during World War II and ended up saving his life. He told me the whole story again, even though he kept it to himself for 60 years prior. He told it well, as usual. Even in his final days, Dad was still the ultimate engaging salesman.

Mom is still with me, and she is as sharp as ever. She still calls me daily. She still calms me down on bad days running Pioneer. She shows up at our office parties and entertains our employees. Most importantly of all, she gets to see the wall I created in our lobby that is a photo tribute and walk down memory lane to the company that she and Dad started in those early days of a postwar America, when a generation came home and started their jobs and careers with a few old-fashioned traditions: hard work and humility toward clients.

I can't put into words how much it means to me that my parents were both around to see and experience the entrepreneurial venture that I undertook. Without their words, sacrifice, dedication and love, I wouldn't have had a chance.

About Frank

Frank J. Cupo, President and Founder of Pioneer Properties, LLC, formed his company in the fall of 1996. Pioneer Properties provides facility management services throughout the United States along with construction management services to major corporations. Since its inception, Pioneer Properties has grown from a start up to a service provider whose client list includes Bank of America, Aeropostale, Ross Stores, HSBC, Quest Labs, Sunrise Assisted Living and Cumberland Farms.

Prior to his forming Pioneer Properties, Frank held management positions in real estate management, development and the commercial construction industry. He was in charge of a commercial real estate portfolio in the northeast for a major real estate developer. Frank's professional experience spans 20 years and also includes commercial real estate finance and commercial construction project management.

Frank holds a Master of Science Degree from New York University specializing in Corporate Real Estate Development. He also holds a Bachelor of Science Degree from Seton Hall University in Business Marketing. His company, Pioneer Properties, is a regular sponsor of the Hackensack Medical Center Tomorrows Children's Fund and POAC (Parents of Autistic Children).

CHAPTER 14

Interview Chat

with John Yodice

———————◆·◆·◆———————

Grace: John, where did you grow up? How big was your family?

John: In Yonkers, New York – born in the Bronx. I have an older brother not in the business; he's a captain in the fire department. No sisters and my mother and father. My father worked 2 jobs: he drove a truck for the Ladies Garment workers Union and evenings he worked at Yonkers Raceway. My mother worked for a housing and urban development agency –locating affordable housing for people.

Grace: As a retailer or restaurateur in our industry – I always love to ask this question. Do you remember the first store you shopped at or the first restaurant you ate in?

John: There was a Woolworth in Yonkers. I remember ordering banana splits because there was a promotion where we had to pop a balloon for the cost of the banana splits! Also there was Jets Hamburger chain, this was before McDonalds came to our town. There weren't many quick serve places to eat, diners were popular then.

Grace: What schools did you attend?

John: Right after high school I went to City College of NY for 2 years, and studied business management. I worked in construction while attending college for a couple of years. At 19, I worked on commercial office buildings as a mason/concrete union worker. It was construction full time. During a heart to heart with my father while, working in construction – coming home tired and spent my father asked "Is that what you want to do for the rest of your life or do you want to be the person who comes to the job with a nice suit and directs what to do?" Basically, be a leader in the construction industry. That's when I decided to go back to college in the evenings and started working with a construction management firm on Long Island building as a project manager building restaurants and shopping centers; we handled surety and insurance projects as well.

Grace: What was your first job in this niche industry?

John: While I was managing a project for a shopping mall – I was approached by someone from Dunkin Donuts to manage construction on their store openings. I worked with them as an owner's rep and managed a region for 11 years. Then I went on to Starbucks starting as a Senior Manager, then getting promoted to Director and staying with Starbucks for 13 years. In those 24 years I was involved with the construction of thousands of stores. When I started with Starbucks in NY – they only had 6 stores in NYC – then I was managing half the country – doing over 300 stores a year. Then I pursued an opportunity with a major drug chain.

Grace: Which was your favorite job in this niche industry?

John: I love my current job the most. I like the smaller box stores because you got to do a lot more, faster! However, I now really enjoy the expansion plans of the boxes I'm building. I love the success, the results of all your hard work! Being involved on the retailer side, I've grown to love the fast pace, the various markets and all the different people you meet. Working with landmark buildings, and flagship locations that will be around for a very long time is very satisfying. Equally rewarding is knowing I was involved with a financially successful project that will be a part of the community for years to come

Grace: So as an industry thought leader, what do you think we're doing great in this industry? What are we excelling in?

John: We are constantly improving; you have to have a certain amount of innovation. With challenges of rental costs and priority locations – these challenges require you to really make sure you're getting the most return on your investment. Innovative design and build out. I've been fortunate to have worked with retailer chains that support the development of the best space possible! And not every company is successful in this.

Grace: What do you think we can improve upon as an industry?

John: There's not one specific item to improve upon. You're thinking should be of continuous improvement – every day with every aspect of your job! View it as a constant improvement challenge. It's an everyday practice!

Grace: If you can wave a magic wand and change one thing in our industry – what would it be?

John: It would be to find a way to pool the highest quality resources together and channel the thinking of your highest quality service providers! Creative, good partners - increase the number of service providers to be valuable partners to the business.

Grace: Do you love what you do?

John: Yes, absolutely!

Grace: How important do you feel it is for a leader – to absolutely love what they do?

John: It is essential for a leader's success. If you're not enjoying what you're doing - how can you be thinking about improving upon it- if you're not loving every aspect of what you're doing?

Grace: What are the top 3 traits you feel make up strong Leadership?

John: First, the ability to promote teamwork (with internal and external partner.) Second, open communication & trust. Be a good listener; be able to hear what's going around you to promote teamwork. And third, be a mentor – to give and receive mentoring. Everyone can use mentoring – you never know it all

Grace: What are the top 3 traits you feel make up strong Teams?

John: Shared vision, communication and trust.

Grace: What is the most important lesson you've learned in this industry that will help someone else along their career path?

John: Don't view the industry with blinders, be open to change and continuous improvement.

Grace: Also, if you had to do it all over again – what, if anything, would you do differently?

John: Nothing. Many of my peers started their career from college and worked their way into the business. I came out of high school, went to college and worked in the field and learned a lot. I was able to relate what I learned in the books, and it taught me a lot with the teams I worked with in the field. It gave me a better sense of realistic expectations. The last thing you want to do is to back someone into the corner to get something done if you don't understand it. Being in the field made me a better leader.

Grace: Who was the most impactful role model or mentor for you? And how have they impacted your career? Your life?

John: My father. Even though he was not in the industry- just seeing how he approached his life. He worked 2 jobs: from 7am-4pm, then 6pm to 11pm, to provide for the family. He never once had a bad attitude and was always positive. He was always happy and smiling. At the time, I didn't realize how important that was. My mother worked full time job, came home, always made dinner each night and was always there for us. If I ever feel bad about anything, I reflect on my life and how I love what I do and I hope it spills over to the people I interact with on a daily basis.

Grace: Are you a role model or mentor for someone else?

John: I hope I am to my family, my team and anyone that I'm responsible for leading. My leadership style is constantly in the teaching and showing mode, sharing best practices not only in the industry but in life.

About John

John Yodice has more than 30 years experience in all aspects of fast paced domestic and international construction, including property management, lease administration, site acquisition and design/build. John first started in the industry in the brick masons union and then progressed onto the concrete workers as a foreman with high rise construction. He attended college while working as an assistant project manager getting his degree in construction and facilities management and eventually was promoted to a project manager managing retail store construction in malls and shopping centers.

After a few years on the contractor side of the business John moved into the owner side for Dunkin Donuts as Construction Manager, shortly thereafter promoted into a senior manager role. He moved on to Starbucks Coffee as Director of Construction and Facilities wherein his 13 years there, he directed over 2000 openings and oversaw the facilities team for the eastern US. Currently John is the Senior Director of Construction for Walgreens. John and his family currently reside in New York.

CHAPTER 15

The Unsung Mentors

by Art Silva

———————◆·◆·◆———————

In my life and career, I have had the good fortune to meet some very talented people who have helped me along the way. Some of those people taught me overtly while others simply set a good example in the way they lived their lives, and I had the opportunity to watch and learn from their leadership styles and see the way they treated others. It is those experiences and teachings that have developed me into the person I am today, and it is my hope that by sharing them, I can help others see just how easy mentorship can be and that even when we may not realize it, we may very well be mentoring someone right now.

My first mentors were both grade-school teachers by profession. They were my parents, and they realized the importance of a good education and gave me a great foundation on which to build. They made huge sacrifices in order to ensure that my three younger siblings and I had excellent opportunities to learn. My parents both worked multiple jobs to take care of the four of us, and while I am sure that it was stressful for them, that stress was never conveyed to us. They both made sure that we had everything we needed to choose the life and career paths that we wanted. They taught me to dream big—not just to acquire material wealth, but to follow my heart. I have tried to imitate as closely as I could their examples of working hard, making sacrifices, being humble, and treating others with respect.

While I might not have realized or appreciated all that I was being taught by my parents, even at an early age I was learning some valuable life and business lessons. I can still remember my father sitting with me when I was young and telling me that it didn't matter whether you were getting paid five dollars an hour or fifty dollars an hour; when you were working, you made sure that you gave that company your best effort. While that might seem like a simple concept, learning that at an early stage in my life helped me build the foundation of a strong work ethic and is a lesson I don't see taught as often as we all would hope.

As time passed and I entered high school, my uncle Vicente stepped in to teach me a lesson in never giving up. Most of my family was born and raised in New Mexico, went to college there, and continued to live there after college, as well. I had always longed to see what life was like outside of New Mexico, so the stories that my relatives would tell me of my uncle helping those who couldn't help themselves and working for a corporation in Florida to help the Hispanic community always intrigued me and made him someone I quietly admired from afar. He eventually moved back to New Mexico and continues to live there and work with a great organization that helps improve the quality of the educational experience for American Indian students through leadership development and mentoring.

The timing of my uncle's move back to New Mexico couldn't have been better. It was my senior year of high school, and college applications were soon due. I had received and submitted all but one, and I was still checking my mailbox every day for that application so that I could finally apply for my dream college. Since this was before the days of online application submissions, when there was still no sign of the application on the day before it was due, I figured that I was out of luck. I had just about given up when my uncle called and said that he would help me. I was certain that there was no way to get the application completed and submitted, but he encouraged me and insisted that we needed to give it a shot if it was something that I really wanted. It was the one place I always wanted to go, so we met at his office and spent the entire night finding the application online, printing it, and cutting and splicing it back together to make it look presentable. He also helped me work through some ideas for the essays in order to make sure that I was completely prepared. It wasn't easy, but with his help I got the application put together, filled out, and postmarked just in time. I am really glad that he encouraged me to strive for what I really wanted because I was accepted to the university, attended, and met my beautiful wife while I was there. I am forever grateful to my uncle not only for teaching me the lesson of working hard and pushing through for something you believe in, but also for helping me reach a goal that changed my life forever.

In what seemed like the blink of an eye, I was nearing graduation from college. It was a time when jobs seemed abundant; the tech boom was in full swing, and as recruiters were visiting, we as soon-to-be graduates realized that we could all be quite picky about which offer we were going to take. By the end of my senior year, I had chosen my career destination and had mapped out all of the milestones from graduation through retirement. I had chosen to go to a large consulting firm where I was sure I would be a manager, senior manager, and partner in record time. At the time, I could tell you exactly when I was going to be married, how many children I was going to have, and when that would happen. I had it all planned out and fully under control - or so I thought.

Shortly after moving to Chicago following my graduation in 2001, I was served a healthy dose of reality. For the first time, I heard the name "Enron" and before long, watched as Andersen closed its doors for good and the tech bubble began to burst. There I was, fresh out of college, realizing that no matter how much we expect life to play by our rules, it doesn't work that way. I found myself in a very scary and lonely place; I had no experience, no backup plan in place, and the job market was tough. I didn't know how to network or ask for help. The city of Chicago was filled with experienced consultants and other people looking for jobs of their own, so it was hard for me to go out there and ask people I didn't know for help. I wasn't aware of the great networking and support system that my university had, so although there were plenty of alumni who I'm sure would have been more than willing to help me, I never made use of that.

When I first learned that my start date at Andersen was being postponed and we were all sure that the Enron story would blow over, I had picked up a part-time job in retail to cover my expenses and keep busy until being called back to work. When the subsequent months passed and it became clearer that the possibility of Andersen's survival was starting to fade away, I decided to take on a store management role, expecting it to be temporary—something to do while I tried to figure out my next career move. Little did I know that what I thought I was taking on as a way to pay the bills while I regrouped my thoughts would ultimately be the industry I now call home. Working in retail had never been something offered for consideration at my college, and it wasn't an industry that anyone I had met was recruiting for. Even if they had, I don't know that I would really have looked into it—it was only by chance that it was where I found myself.

It was in those initial years of my career that I gained a great deal of working knowledge and also started to really understand the importance of a great leader. I was introduced to a regional Vice President whose approach was that of a coach and someone who stood behind her team. She was someone that truly cared about everyone in her region and made us feel like we were special. While working there, I developed a computer program that I thought would be beneficial to the company, but it was only through her insistence and introduction to the CEO that I was able to present it to the right audience and with that, was promoted into the corporate office.

When I moved over to the corporate side of retail, it was as a systems analyst. I was excited that I was immediately given the latitude to work on several big projects which required interaction with several departments and in which I had the opportunity to learn from additional leaders. What I learned then and wished I had known years before was that contrary to what I feared when I started my career, there are a lot of really talented individuals who are more than happy to help pass along their experiences and knowledge just as others had done for them in their past. They were a testament to the fact that even though life gets busy, the best leaders still take the time to develop those around them.

My first career mentors were never formally introduced as such, nor was there any specified program that we followed. In fact, they were simply a few executives who took some time out of their busy days to sit down with me, review my career plans periodically, invite me to meetings to gain experience, and expand my network as they continued to introduce me to others. It was through those interactions that I was able to learn about different areas of the business, develop my own leadership style, and gain a whole new confidence.

I reported to two very experienced and very talented individuals to whom I owe a great deal for believing in me and putting me in the right situations. I also had some great colleagues from whom I learned a lot. One person that I never reported to but who taught me a lot was a vice president with a small but critically important area in the IT department. I always respected how he treated others, but it was when one employee who was then a Director in another area of IT stepped down in title to join his department that I really took notice. It was the respect he showed to others, his willingness to develop his workers, and his honesty that she appreciated enough to take that temporary step back in her career. The role she took turned out to be a great fit, and she became a vital part of the organization. Both of those individuals speak volumes about how important a great leader can be and how sometimes taking a step back in role and changing lanes can ultimately be much more rewarding than just moving forward on the same path.

There have been countless other people who have helped me develop my professional network, have been there to bounce ideas or problems off of, and have coached me in areas I was new to. I would love to be able to mention all of them and describe all of my experiences, but that list would be too lengthy. These have been just a few of the major milestones that have helped shape my life, and I continue to reflect on them when I have to make big decisions. I feel fortunate to have so many examples and experiences to guide me and to have so many wonderful mentors on whom I know I can rely.

So while most people think of mentorship as a formal program—and it is great that formal mentorship programs exist and help to define the roles each person will play—those are not the only mentorship opportunities out there. If you want to become a mentor, take a minute to look around and identify some future talent that simply needs guidance from someone with experience. We were all new to business at one point, and if we try hard enough, we can certainly remember when it all seemed very intimidating. Sometimes a friendly face showing us the way was exactly what we needed to boost our confidence and make us stronger. Let's reach out to those around us who might benefit from our help—or at the very least, remember that as a leader, eyes are always on us and we should set an example for those who are trying to base their leadership styles on what they see from us.

About Art

After earning his Bachelor of Business Administration from the University of Notre Dame, Art Silva began his career in information technology. When an apparent setback changed his plans, he instead began his retail career as a part-time sales associate and decided to approach the career shift as an opportunity. Advancing into store management, he used his computer programming background to create operational efficiencies in labor scheduling ultimately leading to his corporate career in Loss Prevention and Operations where he was promoted into Director and Vice President roles. Realizing that the roots of his success can be traced back to the opportunities he was offered along the way, Art helped develop a networking group of technical professionals and created their mentorship program as a way to start giving back. Seeing the people he is mentoring grow both personally and professionally is what drives him to continue seeking ways to help others achieve their greatest potential.

CHAPTER 16

Interview Chat

with Geno DiSarcina

Grace: Geno, let's start with a bit of your background. Where did you grow up?

Geno: Billerica, Massachusetts.

Grace: How big was your family?

Geno: I am the eldest of 4 kids. I have two brothers and one sister.

Grace: Do you remember the first store you shopped at or the first restaurant you ate in?

Geno: We would do our BTS shopping at The Burlington Mall, but I don't remember what stores were there back then, they were definitely less of them. We would go to a local pizza joint called The Hungry Tiger or a family style place called Lums, but nothing was better than Sunday dinners at my Nana's house!

Grace: What schools did you attend?

Geno: I went to Billerica Memorial High School, Middlesex Community and Westfield State College. I graduated with a BS in Business Management, Marketing.

Grace: What was your first job in this niche industry?

Geno: I started at a reprographics and mailroom outsourcing company. Originally, I was supposed to learn the business from the bottom up, so that I would be able to work in their marketing department. However, the company was sold to Pitney Bowes, so I ended up being a Supervisor of mail/fax services in a large Boston law firm. It was basically like corporate facilities, it just wasn't called it at the time. I then moved on and worked in store facilities. They are very similar as both customers are very demanding; the only difference I see is that with stores it's all on the phone or via email. While with corporate you are on site and work directly with your customer, which is good since you can see the finished product. There's a great satisfaction in actually seeing that the job was well done.

Grace: Which was your favorite job in this niche industry?

Geno: The one I have right now J.Crew, because this is where I got into store facilities (repairs/maintenance) for retail locations. In corporate facilities, I worked with a lot of law firms. I enjoy the retail aspect because it's always changing…I enjoy the energetic pace! I direct all facilities in our main office and stores. Including some remodels for both and just now working a bit with the DC's too. The best projects I've had to do have been with J.Crew. I recently did an executive remodel over the holidays and completed an additional floor (80K sqft) for the home office. I partner with design team and construction on many of these larger projects. Partnering up always ensure we get it done right and to the "current" standards.

Grace: How would you describe the ideal service provider?

Geno: Our best, ideal service provider delivers immediate response. The retailer's expectation is immediate. They need to be on it and keep communication open with constant updates: i.e.: we got the service call, we're on it. Then follow up status: tech will be there in 15 minutes; tech is on site, etc…the information always needs to be current. You have to find service providers that can do this. Generally service providers will do less to keep their costs down – but today we are all asking them to do more. They are using more and more technology to keep their per job costs down. Most are integrated with facilities software so they don't need to type or cut and paste from one system to another. On our side, the coordinators are vigilante; they're bull dogs with providers. We have created "on-boarding" requirements for service providers, so they understand the expectations. A big item is that service providers have to ensure that when account managers go on vacation– they need to train other account managers so Customer Service (to us) isn't affected.

Grace: As an industry thought leader, what do you think we're doing great in our field? What are we excelling in?

Geno: Using technology for tracking and budgeting. We started using a third party technology platform over ten years ago. We were one of the pioneers to start utilizing this. The technology company used their platform for the stores to submit work orders to vendors/our team. Our team and stores could track service calls in real time. We have expanded this technology to our home office, where we use it as well. Additionally, other departments (HR, Loss Prevention, POS, Help Desk, etc…) have begun using it for store requests. This helps us audit calls and has helped us compare different vendors in each trade by completion time, cost, response time etc…which has helped us improve service and decrease average work order costs.

Grace: What do you think we can improve upon as an industry?

Geno: Bench marking and partnerships. We don't benchmark enough. We're working with our facilities technology service provider because there should be a way to check our performance to like retailers- cost per work order and other measurables for repair, plumbing, etc... And keep anonymity. It's important to know how you stand across the industry with other retailers; especially, in these financial times when we are constantly trying to save expense dollars. This would help you pick the right trades to go after...you wouldn't waste time with a trade that you were already below industry average. Concentration on the above average trades would give you more bang for your buck.

Grace: If you can wave a magic wand and change one thing in our industry – what would it be?

Geno: Middle of night calls! Ha! Secondly, the needs for my teams to double check and verify work to ensure vendors are being honest. There are too many opportunities for invoices to be paid when work wasn't done completely or at all. If we didn't need to do this (which I doubt will ever happen) then our teams could get so much more done.

Grace: Do you love what you do?

Geno: Absolutely!

Grace: How important do you feel it is for a leader – to absolutely love what they do?

Geno: It's very important for a leader to love what they do. If you don't have the passion and love for your job - as a leader you can't get others to be passionate about it.

Grace: What are the top 3 traits you feel make up strong Leadership?

Geno: 1. Passion – because you can't lead people unless you believe 100% in what you are doing. I want my team to care about the facilities in the stores and getting the job done. The reason they're so great at is that they share the same passion that I have to get stuff done for stores.

2. Decisiveness. There are people that are indecisive. Most people need 5 or 6 people (some that really don't even need to be involved) to give them the OK to move forward. That type of CYA attitude slows down repairs/maintenance and can cost you valuable down time in a store. I feel fortunate here that I can be accountable for my budget and to trust that it is known that I am getting it done quickly, at right price and with quality. Sometimes it's better to ask for forgiveness than permission. Get decisive. Those are times you may have to change or modify your decision – and that's ok – but just make one first. I empower my team to make decisions.

3. Honesty. There are many way to look at this. I.E. Face mistakes head on, notify your boss immediately. Not telling the truth leads to more not telling the truth. It's simple: things break – we fix it. Sometimes when it doesn't work out – just address it - but be honest about it. Same with team performances, there's no hidden agendas, they will appreciate it and they become loyal to you.

Grace: What are the top 3 traits you feel make up strong teams?

Geno: 1. Communication – the ability to speak openly to each other.

2. The desire to go the extra mile and not settle for less than best.

3. The ability to put the team goal, the company goal ahead of their personal goals.

Grace: What is the most important lesson you've learned in this industry that will help someone else along their career path?

Geno: Where there's a will, there's a way. Don't be afraid to fail. Sometimes people are so afraid to fail they don't try. It comes down to making a decision, too. They are afraid of major challenge, when sometimes that is the best thing for you especially if it challenges you mentally. Most issues we deal with are not clear cut or easy to deal with. I have a little reminder taped on my monitor – "Nothing in life is to be feared. It is only to be understood" (Marie Curie) and that sums it up pretty much for me. Pretty funny you'd think that was from Ali or Lombardi. Oh and the other reminder – "Don't Shoot the Messenger" that one of my associates (Lauren) gave me.

Grace: If you had to do it all over again – what, if anything, would you do differently?

Geno: Invested in Apple at the beginning! Ha! I would say that I would have gotten into the facilities world a bit sooner – not stayed in the reprographics/mail business for as long.

Grace: Who was the most impactful role model or mentor for you? How have they impacted your career and ultimately your life?

Geno: My father. He taught me some of the best simple life lessons. Such as - Get in early, stay late. Be a dedicated hard worker

---

it will pay off in the end. Be tenacious and not give up. Always be willing to learn; especially from your mistakes. My father was a history teacher and taught me those lessons growing up. Coming from a very athletic family, my father was a basketball and baseball coach – so we were always very team oriented. I would go to the games to see my father coach. This is all the stuff we need to make sure our video game kids are learning.

Grace: Are you a role model or mentor for someone else?

Geno: I would like to think I am for my team and my children. Only time will tell. As my kids have gone into college – I see it in bits and pieces. I am happy that they've learned some things from me, even if they don't realize it. It's a work in progress – which is a good thing – because they are well rounded. Part of being a mentor is people take the good and bad from you- they learn what to do and what not to do.

Grace: Let's wrap up with your one word to describe this industry and why.

Geno: Dynamic. It's evolving, ever changing. It's always changing with technology and the way we communicate. Ten years ago it took a week to get things done, then it became within a week, then it became 2-3 days, now it's within same day. The expectations are much greater now.

About Geno

Geno DiSarcina has more than 23 years in Facilities Management. He started his career at Pitney Bowes Management Services and Archer Management. He has been with J.Crew since 1995 and is currently the Senior Director of Facilities and Office Services. He empowers his incredible team of 45 and encourages them to GSD (GET STUFF DONE) everyday. One of his favorite quotes is: "Ours is not to reason why. Ours is but to do and die", by Alfred Lord Tennyson. Geno enjoys spending time with his daughter Taylor and son Chris when they are home from college or getting away from it all with Rachel Snow. He's an avid Boston sports fan for all teams.

CHAPTER 17

Leadership: A Different Perspective

By Randall D. Weis

I can remember as a child growing up people referring to "born leaders," usually referring to a person's ancestry and that somehow leadership was in a person's DNA. Often the examples of leadership that I saw were the obvious ones: a military leader, a government official, Gandhi, etc. But leaders are around us every day in every form, and most leaders go unnoticed in life, and many times those leaders evolve and were not "made" or formed by others. They become leaders by challenging the status quo, as was the case with Martin Luther King, Jr.

In my case, I had great mentors growing up with my father and grandfather, who were known for speaking their minds and not following the status quo. Both were quick to let their opinions be known and always listened to the points of view of others, never forcing their opinions on others but letting others rethink their stated positions. Both were able to argue their points of view with their peer groups and were often seen as a voice of reason, and from that they emerged as leaders both in the family and outside of the family.

I remember the first time I really had a chance to be a leader, and this example has followed me throughout my career. After getting my degree in logistics, I wanted to join a professional organization of logistics graduates, and such a group existed on a national level called Delta Nu Alpha. In my Midwest community there was no local chapter of Delta Nu Alpha, so I connected with about a dozen working logistics professionals and invited them to lunch at the cafeteria at my workplace. At that point, since I was the force behind the idea, I prepared an agenda, had some information from the headquarters of Delta Nu Alpha, and ran the meeting. The group decided that we should have a chapter, and in order to get recognized by the national organization, we needed a board of directors, etc., so we held a quick election and I was asked to be the founding president. At the time I was 23—by far, the youngest of the group—but was recognized for seeing a need, organizing others, and bringing things to a vote as to move forward or not. This was my first stage of understanding what leaders do. Today, these same simple principles have formed who I am in every day life.

My life experience as a leader has five foundational items that always reappear in matters where leadership is required. These five pillars are:

1. The urge to explore new territory.

2. The ability to influence.

3. Challenge the status quo.

4. Courage to speak out.

5. Desire to differentiate.

The Urge to Explore

The urge to explore is what stops most from leading. If you don't explore, you can't make a mistake in life. More valuable information comes from the mistakes we make oftentimes than from the successes we have. The only people I have met in life who never make mistakes are those who never take a chance, never explore the unknown, and remain in that safe spot where they can't be criticized. Leaders understand how failure can provide great learning, just like success does.

The Ability to Influence

The ability to influence, the second pillar, can come from many areas and is perhaps the pillar with the greatest mystique. Dale Carnegie wrote the bestseller *How to Win Friends and Influence People* in 1937 and introduced to modern management at that time some simple principles regarding how to influence people. Those principles start with the concept that you have to engage others and win their confidence (friendship) to be able to influence others. Politicians have long understood the importance of influence, as it may be the key determinant as to who gets elected in the end and who does not. The person with the greatest influence is the one who wins in an election. You cannot overlook the importance of how much engaging with others drives your ability to influence.

Challenging the Status Quo

Challenging the status quo is perhaps the riskier pillar to implement. This is where failure has its greatest potential. Midway through my corporate career with a large pharmaceutical company, I accepted a job transfer to a division in Stamford, CT. This division made hair care products, and in our warehouse we had 125 people employed in the process of putting together orders for customers—sometimes 7 days a week, 24 hours a day. This was 1981, and technology and industrial engineering were challenging how things had been done in the past. With the assistance of an outside consultant, we took a look at our workforce productivity and also looked at making a capital investment in new computer-aided order picking processes and ways to make this function less labor-intensive. Our analysis told us that we could eliminate 50 positions if we invested two million dollars in new technology, technology which had never been proven or used yet, but on paper the idea seemed bulletproof. We knew there were several outcomes by challenging the way things had been done for years, and some were very positive, and some potentially career-altering for me. I could have chosen to stay with the status quo, or I could have moved forward with a factory automation program that revolutionized how we ran our warehouse for decades to come. If the project succeeded, our annual savings would have been $2.5 million with a $2 million dollar initial investment, and if it did not work, we would have wasted $2 million and lost the confidence of our workforce and our management. Since I understood the technology being proposed, I did not need 100% assurance to move forward; we made the investment, and with the exception of some start-up issues, the project was a huge success, leading the way for a promotion that soon followed.

The Courage to Speak Out

The courage to speak out is how leaders get the most recognition. Martin Luther King Jr. was known for speaking out with eloquence and is an example that most of us can readily identify with. But speaking out does not always assure that things will work out the way you had hoped, as there are consequences associated with speaking out. King was jailed; other political leaders have fallen on their own swords, as well.

In my last corporate position before starting my own business, I was the head of corporate real estate for my firm. The firm was nearing the end of a lease on our corporate headquarters, and my role was to put together a strategy for the next 20 years as to where our corporate staff would be located and what was in the best interest of the shareholders first and employees second. To accomplish this, we hired a well-known real estate consulting firm, looked at the demographics of our workforce, and looked at what functions needed to be in New York City and which ones might be suitable to locate in more urban, less expensive areas. Throughout this process, we took a blank sheet of paper approach and decided to be open to a compete relocation or just stay where we were for another 20 years. After an exhaustive one-year study, we presented our results to our senior leadership, and my immediate supervisor was irate at our findings. Our findings were that we needed to split the corporate functions and take 80% of them out of New York City, and keep 20% or fewer of the senior leadership in midtown Manhattan.

So the day finally came, and the consultants and I made our recommendation to the EVP of the company, who got very angry with the conclusions. First, we failed to factor in that the EVP had just bought an expensive apartment on Central Park West, was friends socially with our building owner and his comrades in top management—about a dozen or so—liked walking to work on nice days down Park Avenue... All of that had not been factored in. Being a bit of a novice, I thought our responsibility was to our shareholders first, as the new lease would be approximately $1 billion, and second to our employees, who every day were trying to save the company money in their jobs—but we missed the point. The point was that a company with 50,000 people does not make a decision like this for the greater good; it was more about feeding into the needs/habits of the top dozen people. We knew some of this going in, but felt that we needed to speak out, as this was an issue the firm would have to live with for the next 20 years. In the end, I stepped down in nine months, the company proceeded with a status quo direction of keeping things as they were, just giving the landlord a new lease, and the consultant collected their fee. Three years later, the EVP was fired, and the company split up their real estate and followed the strategy that was proposed.

I learned a valuable and expensive lesson. When you are in a corporate environment, doing the right thing has consequences. Standing up for what is right has consequences. At the end of the day, everyone knew what was right and everything got righted for the company. I on the other hand, decided I was born to lead, not follow, so I started my own business. For many, following is easy; for me, it was never an option.

Desire to be Different

The desire to be different takes on many forms, but is in part about being noticed in a positive way. Being different for the sake of being different is not always successful.

One of the things I saw watching my father work at his white-collar job in the '50s and '60s was that he did several things differently than others in our neighborhood. He was always early to work—usually an hour before everyone else—getting things situated for the day, trying to do more than the next person. Likewise, he was not bristling at the end of the day to run out the door, as there was always something else to do to separate him from the pack. Dad had a tan leather briefcase he carried every day with paperwork and reading material, and often, when not traveling, would spend time at night at the kitchen table going over things and taking care of mundane items like filling out his expense report—something I am sure his colleagues did on "company time" at their desks. Dad also kept up some basic appearances: white shirt, tie, dark suit, every day—hardly the most practical thing for a person working in an auto factory, but that was part of his brand and he wanted to represent himself as a professional. Every Sunday night, Dad shined his work shoes so that he started the week out with his best foot forward. The following Sunday, the shoes and the shoe shine kit came out.

When I began working, I did some things to be different, as well. I noticed that when I got my first job, the VP who interviewed me, a Harvard MBA, wore cuff links every day, wore starched shirts and always looked like a million bucks. Later I would learn that how you present yourself is an important door opener in the business world. If you look the part, you automatically remove some roadblocks when dealing with the leadership of most companies. Today, I know before I go to bed what I am wearing the next day based on who I am seeing, and I always have an eye for being dressed equally to or better than everyone I am meeting that day. In John Malloy's famous book Dressing for Success, he talks about how the right combination of classic dress sets the tone when you meet someone. I read this book when I was 20 years old, and the principles are with me today.

Being different is more than how you dress. It is attitude, the ability to look at a minority point of view on an issue, listening more than talking, and not rushing to judgment when the rest of the world is doing so.

In my company, we have a group of people who clean carpets in corporate office buildings at night. Sometimes a client will call us and accuse our men of taking something the night before or turning a radio dial to a different station in someone's cubicle. These complaints get reported to our salespeople, and they are escalated to me. I always make sure that I have the full story (yes, customers are not always right) before I judge my own people or accuse them of something. More often that not, these complaints are unfounded.

I have had the good fortune to meet with and work with many great leaders over my career. None stands out larger than Roger Milliken, who was Chairman of the Board of the Milliken Textile and Chemical Company almost until his death at age 92. Mr. Milliken, as he is known by his employees, had a building fire in 2004 that eliminated his entire US carpet production capability, reported to be at that time a $150 million-a-year business. The plant and warehouse was roughly one million square feet, and was one of the largest employers in the town of La Grange, GA, an hour or so south of Atlanta. The fire started as a result of an equipment malfunction, but by the time the first responders could arrive, the entire facility was a total loss. Within hours, Mr. Milliken was on the site himself surveying the ruins, getting an update on the safety of his employees, and having conversations with a general contractor who had built other plants for him about getting going rebuilding the factory. Twenty-four hours later, Mr. Milliken addressed the media and said the following:

1. First and foremost, there were no injuries to any of the responders or his associates.

2. No one would lose his job, as he needed to transfer some workers overseas where other plants were, and would need the rest to work on the rebuilding efforts.

3. He also said that in a way, the loss of the factory gave them an opportunity to rebuild a new plant far superior in technology, etc., than the old one.

It was reported that the insurance deductible against the loss was about $10 million, and here stood the chairman of the board stating all of the positives and looking toward the future with great optimism. This is how leaders lead!

Leaders are not born. Name one born leader, and I will challenge your findings. Leadership is not DNA-driven; it is environmental, and is around us every day. Those that keep an open mind, look at the success traits and patterns of others, and have the influencing ability that Dale Carnegie talks about will rise to the top.

About Randy

In 1990, Randy's strong entrepreneurial spirit and keen industry vision culminated in the launch of his own full-service flooring maintenance company serving the commercial market. His extensive experience in various management positions with a major international pharmaceutical company, coupled with industry affiliations—Randy was a founding member of the Delta Nu Alpha Transportation Fraternity (Cincinnati, OH), founder and first president of the Association of Interstate Commerce Commission Practitioners and president of the National Council of Physical Distribution Managers—had yielded extensive industry resources and a solid background in facilities management.

A graduate of the University of Cincinnati with a Bachelor of Science degree in Business Logistics and Instructor of Logistics and Curriculum Advisor at the same institution, Randy was the youngest person on record to be admitted to practice before the Interstate Commerce Commission at the age of 20.

After the launch of RD Weis Companies, he quickly recognized the benefits of working with manufacturer-specified cleaning programs and established a relationship with Milliken, one of the world's leading textile manufacturers. In 1996, he formalized his company's successful relationship with Milliken by becoming an authorized MilliCare® Commercial Carpet Care franchisee, and then focused on expanding RD Weis Companies' range of product and service offerings.

Randy shares his industry expertise while playing an active role in multiple industry, civic and cultural associations. He is the sitting Chairman of the StarNet® Commercial Flooring Co-operative (where he also served two terms as Director); Board Member of the Muscular Dystrophy Association; Board Member of the Fairfield Arts Council; past Board Member of IFMA, Hudson Valley Chapter; and past Board Member and Director of Membership of IFMA, Connecticut Chapter.

A frequent contributor to industry publications, Randy has been quoted in and written articles for a variety of publications including *Crain's New York Business, New York Real Estate Journal, Cleaning & Maintenance Management, Today's Facility Manager, Facilities Design & Management, Better Buildings, Carpet & Rug Industry and Real Estate New York*.

CHAPTER 18

Interview Chat

with Paula Settanni

Grace: Where did you grow up? How big was your family?

Paula: I grew up in a small town in South Jersey, Haddonfield, just outside Philadelphia

Grace: Do you remember the first store you shopped at or the first restaurant you ate in?

Paula: I don't remember the first store but the town I grew up in has a nice main street with little shops, as kids we use to ride our bikes down town and buy little toys and candy –

Grace: What schools did you attend?

Paula: Catholic University in Washington DC for under grad and grad school. I have a Bachelor's in Architecture and a Master's in Engineering – both with a concentration in construction management

Grace: What was your first job in this niche industry?

Paula: In college, I interned for a small GC/millwork company doing misc construction management tasks. Then I worked for a large GC. My job was on site and I was responsible for updating the drawings in the job trailer with all of the RFI responses, changes and clarifications.

Grace: Which was your favorite job in this niche industry?

Paula: My second job out of grad school, I worked in Philadelphia for Gilbane Building Company. I was an office engineer working on rolling out a program management job for a bank renovation with locations in Philadelphia and New Jersey. I learned so much there, to really build a foundation on, I worked with great people and for my first real mentor, Lisa. I really liked the company and the management. The position also helped me determine what I liked about the industry. I am still in touch with a number of executives and co-workers from Gilbane. And the position I just left, the US Facility Manager for IKEA. It was just the perfect combination of all the aspects of the industry; it's strategic yet I still have the opportunity to manage projects and people. I am continually challenged and always learning. In addition to being surrounds by great co-workers, I feel really lucky to have this opportunity to work for such a great company with strong ethics. I am adjusting to my new role with IKEA as the Global Facility Management Service Delivery Manager.

Grace: As an industry thought leader, what do you think we're doing great in this industry? What are we excelling in?

Paula: Developing and bringing awareness to the Facility Management role and bringing the importance of maintaining assets through a proactive preventive maintenance program to top level executives. The impact a good facility management program has on a company's bottom line is significant and it can be a positive impact if the company chooses to manage it correctly.

Grace: What do you think we can improve upon as an industry?

Paula: There is so much happening in the industry with technology, benchmarking, FM degrees and certifications and various industry organizations, the only thing I can say is to provide more information faster! Facility Management is evolving and headed in such a positive direction, it is great to be a part of the change.

Grace: If you can wave a magic wand and change one thing in our industry – what would it be?

Paula: Wow, I don't know, I guess more of the awareness I spoke about earlier, the role that Facilities plays for any business is key. When companies and executives understand the FM concept and you have that support from management it completely changes the way business decisions are made and the FM program execution. Maintenance becomes a proactive program that is recognized, planned for, incorporated into the business plan and leveraged across multiple locations instead of becoming a series reactive repairs and independent projects that negatively impact the bottom line.

Grace: Do you love what you do?

Paula: I definitely have a passion for what I do. I wouldn't say I like all the aspects or tasks, but working toward the ultimate goal of implementing an FM Program and seeing the changes and impact along the way, achieving that goal is what I love and that is really great sense of accomplishment. I love architecture and buildings and this is a positive way to impact them and be involved in the industry.

Grace: What are the top 3 traits you feel make up strong Leadership?

Paula: First I would say, someone who can lead change. This requires many traits, it is easier to lead something that is established then to lead a significant change. Some traits or abilities I think are important to lead change are being a self starter who is able to establish a clear vision and direction. Communicate effectively; explain why change is needed and how it impacts the business, customers and the employees. Having the ability to think things through and consider various scenarios and outcomes and the ability to re-evaluate along the way and adjust if necessary in order to achieve the goal. Providing the necessary guidance and support through the entire change process even through mistakes and rough times and of course, celebrating the accomplishments - taking responsibility, regardless of the outcome.

Second, a strong leader is someone who has empathy and respect for each team member. Understanding each team member, acknowledging their value and contribution will allow the leader to provide the correct support, set each member up to succeed; and more importantly motivate, inspire and bring out the best in them. I am a big believer in understanding someone and letting someone do what they are good at, giving them the freedom to do things their own way, make mistakes and be challenged to correct it when things do not go as anticipated. When a leader is connected to each member in this way and invests in them, the return will be evident. The team will be engaged and in turn support the leader and they are on the right path to success.

And third, honesty, values, integrity; I think that speaks volumes for itself. Without this your team will never have trust in you.

Grace: What are the top 3 traits you feel make up strong Teams?

Paula: One, motivation with an open attitude and willingness to learn. Two, responsibility and sense of ownership to perform their role well and respect the roles and work of others. And three, to support team members and realize that recognition and success comes when the entire team succeeds

Grace: **What is the most important lesson you've learned in this industry that will help someone else along their career path?**

Paula: I don't know that it is specific to this industry; I think it applies to any industry. You know about your industry and of course are always learning new things and aspects of your job, stay true to yourself, have confidence in your ability and be open to learning another way of doing things.

Grace: **If you had to do it all over again – what, if anything, would you do differently?**

Paula: Nothing I can think of. I think everything happens for a reason so I would not do anything differently. I've learned from things that haven't turned out so well or how I wanted them to. Even if it is learning what you don't want, what situations you don't want to be in and what type of people you don't want to be around. One thing I do differently now is I take initiative and act sooner when my instincts or gut feelings tell me something is not right. I do not wait to see how things turnout or rely on others to do the right thing or act appropriately. Your values and integrity should not be compromised, if something doesn't feel right, act on it, as long as you stay true to that, there is no reason to do anything differently. I have had some significant mentors in my career that through leading by example, with strong values and integrity, provided a good frame work for me. When I look back on my career, I can clearly identify three mentors. I often find myself asking, what 'would this person do', 'how would they handle this' or 'what questions would they ask me.' I think if I had to pick something to do differently, I would want to realize the impact they had on me sooner and take advantage of their leadership by asking more questions and observing everything they did and how they handled every situation. Luckily, I still have contact with them, even though it is not as often as I would like. I have made it a point to communicate to each of them that they were mentors to me and they have influenced me and my career. My most recent mentor retired, so I took advantage of that as much as possible before he moved on – lesson learned!

Grace: Who was the most impactful role model or mentor for you? How have they impacted your career or your life?

Paula: As I mentioned, I have three, all three have the qualities I mentioned in a good leader. Of course they have many other qualities as well but these were consistent and have significance for me. When I am uncertain or lose my way I go back to the things they taught me.

For example there was my manager Lisa at Gilbane. She was involved in my initial career development. She took an interest in me and believed and supported me throughout our time working together. She was a stronger leader that managed every part of the program we implemented. She touched every aspect, the people, the process, she really had knowledge of everything. She set the direction for everything down to what would transpire in a meeting, she knew exactly how a client would respond. She also had a great ability to re-evaluate and redirect the program or meeting if necessary, she made it all so simple and clear. She was also exceptional at connecting with people and could quickly determine an accurate read on anyone and knew how to work with them immediately.

Then, there was Dan, my manager at Macys, he was always so calm and in control, he was really a true leader. He lead change in such an honest and positive way and had an ability to think things though, ask the right questions then provide a well thought out objective answer and direction. It was amazing. He took an interest in everyone and connected with each person in a different way. I was so impacted by my time working for him that I actually sent him an email a few years after working for him telling him about the qualities I took away from my experience with him. I was working with him on 9/11 in New York, he asked me to walk around the block with him later that day, I didn't want to go for obvious reasons, but I felt ok walking with him, if anyone else asked me to do that I probably would have said no.

And finally, my previous manager at IKEA. Gary always seems to know the right thing to do; he is honest and has strong values. You always know where you stand with him. If he is happy with you, he lets you know, if he is not happy, you know that too. But he doesn't make you feel bad, he just talks you though ways to do it better the next time and he moves on. He challenges but supports his team one hundred percent in any situation. He is exceptional at establishing a clear direction, breaking things down into simple terms and leading everyone to achieve goals. His leadership and example have gotten me to a point when I say 'I need to talk to you it's really important.' I explain my plan and when I am finished I ask, 'is this ok?' and he laughs and says 'yes, it's fine, you don't need me for this.' I am figuring things out, developing plans and making decisions he agrees with but without his direct input. He knows that sometimes when I say I need to talk to him, it really means 'I' literally need to do the talking and he just needs to listen and give me the assurance it is ok. He genuinely cares for and connects with his team, I feel lucky to work for someone with his level of competence, leadership ability and values.

Grace: Are you a role model or mentor for someone else?

Paula: I don't know! I would hope I have provided some insight to others along the way. I can tell you two instances where I realized I had impacted employees and realized they valued and learned something from me.

I had an employee call me a few years after we had worked together, he said 'I am calling to tell you about what I told my employee about you today. It made me think about what I learned from you and wanted to let you know.' Now it really wasn't a big deal because it had to do with printing a document. He told me he would become so annoyed when I would ask him to print something so we could review it. So today when he asked his employee to print a document and he found some issues he realized why I use to do it and wanted to tell me. It wasn't actually about the printing, it was more about a way of working and why, I realized that I had positively impact someone so much so that he called to tell me about it.

In the second situation, I was working a little late and one of my employees was with me, she pulled her chair up to my desk and said 'Can I talk to you about something? I really trust your opinion and I don't know what to do and I know you will know what to do.' I immediately thought that something happened with work and couldn't imagine why she was so serious, it turned out she had a question about a personal situation. I gave her the best advice I could and talked about different scenarios with her. I was really taken back and flattered that she would ask me about something personal. I realized at that time that I not only impacted her professionally but she also felt comfortable and wanted my advice personally as well. I realized my actions, influence or opinions had an impact both in and outside of work.

Actually, now that I think about it, another instance happened just a few months ago, I was walking through the office with another co worker who is probably in her twenties, I don't know her too well, we only worked on one project together. We were just talking about work, travel, shopping, nothing really significant and she turned to me, smiled and said 'When I grow up, I want to be just like you.' I was kind of shocked but I just smiled, laughed and said 'thank you.' Specifically why she said it, I have no idea, but the fact that I inspired someone to want achieve something, whatever it is, she thought it was important, it was really the ultimate compliment.

Grace: What's the one word that best describes your career in this industry and why?

Paula: Evolving. From one job to the next everything has just evolved. From project to project, one step to the next, everything was just logical and came with a broader scope; it was a seamless transition that just evolved. If someone ever told me 20 years ago, I would be creating a global FM strategy and delivery scope, negotiating global FM agreements and managing global projects; I would have never believed them.

About Paula

Paula Settanni, has over nineteen years of experience in construction, facility and program management, specifically in the retail industry. She has helped retailers develop facility management programs on both national and global levels. An active IFMA and PRSM member, Paula has contributed to industry publications such as PRSM Magazine and Retail Facility Business. Paula works diligently to help the Facility Management industry grow by sharing best practices, participating in industry programs and networking to bring qualified and experienced vendors together with retailers looking to grow their Facility Management Program.

Paula has worked for a number of large, well known retailers such as Macy's, Inc. and IKEA, Property, Inc., She has held a wide range of responsibility including new construction, remodels, special projects, facility management and energy management and procurement on the national level. Currently, Paula works for IKEA Services AB/IKEA Group Property Inc. in Sweden as the Global Facility Management Service Delivery Manager responsible for development and implementation of global strategies and projects across the organization and for acquisition, mobilization and monitoring of global agreements. Paula holds a Bachelor's of Science Degree in Architecture and a Master's of Science Degree in Engineering, both with a concentration in Construction Management from The Catholic University of America in Washington, DC.

CHAPTER 19

Learning to Lead

By Jeff Matthews

I've learned many leadership skills in my life, some by trial and error. I have done my best to adapt these skills to my style of leadership and to apply them throughout my career. This story is an experience that influenced me more than I ever realized. At the time, I didn't even really understand what I was doing, but it has made a large impact on my life and career ever since.

In college, like many students, I was confused about where my career would lead. I really didn't even understand what the word career meant. I decided during my sophomore year to coach a basketball team of eight-year-old boys. At the time, it was just something fun to do. I had been somewhat of a leader in my past, but only by example. I had never stood up in front of a group of people and actually tried to inspire someone. That thought had never even occurred to me as I made the decision to coach. I was good at basketball, and that seemed to be the only criterion for coaching in my mind. Little did I know, this experience would mold me as a leader for the rest of my life.

I inherited "The Heat," a team of eight-year-old boys that had never won a basketball game. They were 0-10 the year before. It's amazing how a record like that can influence children. They didn't know what it meant to win, and they certainly didn't expect to win. I quickly noticed that each child only wanted the ball so that he could shoot a basket. That was their only expectation. Practices started out with crying and arguing over the ball. Once I realized what the problem was, I decided to focus on teaching the kids the basics of basketball and the fundamentals of footwork. I figured the less I taught about shooting, the less they would think about it. The team was receptive and listened well, and as a result, we won our first three games. Although we were winning, the players still had a "me first" attitude. Each player still wanted to score points and would get frustrated if he didn't get the ball. To my surprise, winning did not seem to be helping our team.

Game four: We faced the Bulls, a team that had not lost a game in two years. Although we had won our first three games just like the Bulls, my players lacked confidence. Before the game, my team did nothing but talk about how good the Bulls were and how bad the Bulls would beat us that night. And, in fact, they did. They beat us as bad as eight-year-olds can beat eight-year-olds. The game was never even close. After the loss, I was angry and I knew that I had to change my team's attitude. After all, these were eight-year-old children. How could one team of eight-year-olds be so much better than my team? It was clear to me that our loss wasn't about experience or dramatically different skill levels; it was about attitudes and confidence levels.

During our first practice after the loss, I made it clear to the team that I was not happy with their performance on the court and that I was angry about their attitude before the game. As most basketball coaches do for discipline, I made the team run laps. I was very clear that this was for attitude, not for losing. I made expectations for attitude on our team. All players must keep their heads high, respect one another, and expect to win. Over the next several weeks we went 2-3, and I realized for the first time that teaching these children how to win was more important than teaching them basketball. I realized that I had the opportunity to influence them for life. I continued to focus on attitude, trying to make winners out of this team and still teaching the fundamentals of the game. I taught the importance of rebounding, defense, and passing. Shooting was reduced to the end of practice. I emphasized all phases of the game and helped each player further develop the skills that they were best at. The best rebounders focused on rebounding, the best ball handlers focused on ball handling, and so on. Soon each player was gaining confidence because of his success at practice and during the games. They no longer complained about not shooting the ball because they knew that the shots would come if they continued to develop and focus on their skill sets.

Game 10: The final game of the season. Our record was 5-4 versus the 9-0 Bulls. Our team was hyped up and feeling confident. Each of the players was saying, "We're going to beat the Bulls! We're going to win! We're going to stomp 'em!" Seeing this made me so proud as a coach and leader. I had inspired them. This was our shot! Everything I had taught them was evident before the game.

At the beginning of the fourth quarter, the game was tied at 29-29. No team had been this close to beating the Bulls. Confidence and anxiousness was all over the faces of the players. Each player always got equal playing time on my team. Zac (our best player) had already played his minutes for the game. With the chance to win on the line, the whole team started saying, "Coach, put Zac in, put Zac in! If Zac plays, we can win the game!"

As I gathered the team into a huddle, I told them that if I put Zac back in the game, then someone else wouldn't get to play.

Then I asked the question, "Who is willing to give up their playing time?" The whole team got quiet, and then Brian, the most selfish player on the team, raised his hand and said, "Coach, I'll sit out if you put Zac in." At that moment, I realized what I had done: I had created a team. Faced with the decision to put Zac in, I contemplated the consequences. We may have had a real chance to win if I decided to let Zac play the fourth quarter. We might have been able to win with Brian in the game; he had played well, too, and he had worked so hard to become a better player and teammate all season. In thinking it over, I realized that I had to continue teaching the lesson that I had worked so hard to embed in their minds all season. So, without Zac in the lineup, the team hit the floor and gave it their best effort.

I would love to write here that we won the game, but we didn't. We lost by four points (by far, the closest any team had come to beating the Bulls). As the team came off the court, I expected them to be disappointed and upset, but it was the complete opposite. Their heads were high; they were confident and they were happy. I realized the victory at that moment. We didn't win the game—we won teamwork, we won confidence, we won pride! The team was doing what I had expected and taught them to do: They were keeping their heads high and showing confidence. This new attitude carried us to two undefeated seasons in the next two years. That included beating the Bulls in both seasons.

It was so important for these players to understand the goal. The goal was not to shoot the ball; it was to win the game. I realize now this concept is so simple that even an eight-year-old can understand it. Complete focus has to be given to the ultimate goal. I also needed to teach them what it meant to win so that they could better understand what it meant to lose. Success is so important, and until you experience success in your ultimate goals, you really don't understand failure. Failure hurts so much more after you have experienced success. Winning the first three games was important so that they could comprehend the feeling of losing. The losses did not hurt as much until the team really understood teamwork and the goal of winning.

I realized throughout this experience that knowing each player individually and understanding his skill set was critical, as well. This helped each player gain confidence in himself and his particular skill set. Each small successes in practice and during the games added to each player's confidence. I had to teach them how important each facet of the game was and how it affected the outcome with a win or loss. Brian, for example, was a really good defender but not a good shooter. As he focused on defense, he began to expand his game and gained tremendous confidence. Stealing a pass led to easy lay-ups for him. More importantly, he realized the importance of his defensive skills because I always had him guard the best player on the other team. My best rebounder decided he didn't even care to shoot. It became his goal to get the most rebounds in each game, and he only cared to shoot if he got an offensive rebound under the basket. I was able to convey to these players that each of these moving parts made up the machine. Not everyone can score, but everyone can do his part to help our team win. As each player began to appreciate his own skill set, the players also began to appreciate their teammates' individual skill sets. At this point, the team was born.

I've learned a lot from this experience and many more throughout my life. There are things that I learned from my coaching experience that I still implement today in my professional career. I instill the importance of teamwork, confidence, excitement, and the desire to succeed. Each day will not go as you plan—and each day will not always bring what you want it to—but in the end, you still strive for success.

About Jeff

Jeff Matthews is an expert in retail design and construction management. During Jeff's career he has been responsible for new and remodel stores totaling over 500 stores in the North American Region. He was hired at his current position, Manager, Retail Store Development, to develop a franchise design and construction program for Pandora Jewelry in the North American Region. Jeff won "Best Overall Performance, Retail 2011" at Pandora while implementing brand consistency and overseeing the openings of 73 retail stores in 2011. He has retail experience at companies such as HUE Studio, Belk, The Body Shop, Rack Room Shoes and Off Broadway Shoe Warehouse. Jeff spent his time at HUE Studio overseeing the development and implementation of a brand new retail concept in women's leggings and hosiery. While at The Body Shop, Jeff was Manager of Design and Construction for North America where he was responsible for aligning global design into his region and working to further develop the design for all global stores. During his time at The Body Shop, Jeff's department was recognized as "Design Department of the Year" by Retail Construction Expo. Before his career in retail Jeff worked as a teacher in Technology Education where he won Technology Teacher of the Year for North Carolina. Jeff also led his Technology Student Association to National Chapter of the Year twice in four years. Currently, Jeff resides in Charlotte, North Carolina with his wife Melissa and two daughters Nia Addison and Olivia Jane and enjoys playing "baby dolls" with his girls.

CHAPTER 20

Interview Chat

with Steve Kitezh

Grace: Where did you grow up? How big was your family?

Steve: I grew up in different areas of Brooklyn. I'm the oldest with one brother and one sister. My father was always in the garment industry. He worked for shops that mass produced garments for department stores. He became very good at what he did. First it was sewing then he was hired by firms to take sample clothing to reconstruct and value engineer the manufacturing of apparel. My mother remained a house wife after she was married. Before marriage she was a night club singer, she always loved to sing but gave it up for family because she wanted that more than an entertainment career. My grandfather on my mother's side had a trucking business and did most of his work in the Bowery. Before that my Grandfather was eager to get into army at the age of 17 and fought in WW1.

Grace: Do you remember the first store you shopped at or the first restaurant you ate in?

Steve: The most important store was A&S on Fulton Street in Brooklyn. From an early age the greatest thrill was to take the elevators from the 1st floor to the 6th floor. The elevators were the fastest in the city and that would make your stomach feel as if it stayed on the first floor.

Grace: What schools did you attend?

Steve: I always had a passion for design and creativity since I was 6 or 7 years old. I had the ability to build and create things using observation and innate skill. Growing up in Brooklyn with a working class family the creativity was appreciated because my mom loved that I fixed things. Architecture and design was not supported. Ultimately I studied speech and language therapy through graduate school publishing a thesis on aphasia. It was about logical language errors aphasics made on a standardized language test. I attended the City University of New York. I also worked at NY Veteran Hospital for 2 years which was helpful to this.

Grace: How did you get started in this industry?

Steve: My first job in Speech Therapy was at the NY Veteran's Hospital as a paid intern. But while I was pursing that professionally, my hobby was composing piano music. That is how I met my friend Pat. I bought a piano she was selling from an ad she placed in a newspaper. Pat was an actress in a theatre club and encouraged me to join. I became the club's lighting technician, but also built sets and had occasional acting roles there. This experience was both creative and visual. When I graduated from college with a degree in speech and language therapy I was eager to get a job in the field – but at the time jobs were limited because there was a recession in the health care industry. I was on staff at Brooklyn College for one year, as part on the master's program but got discouraged because I could not find a job after graduation and decided to leave the field to pursue something that involved the creativity I enjoyed at my old theater club. I found an odd job with CBS - building sets for a magazine. I stayed there for 2 years and concluded that I liked the design business better than working at a speech clinic – because actual clinical work was more about issuing reports that justified future budgets than being effective to the patient.

Grace: Which was your favorite job in this industry?

Steve: At CBS – I really enjoyed working with a variety of designers on feature stories such as making a kitchen 4 ways, or procuring accessories for stylists to use when photographing food or interiors. Then I went on to Walker Group, a design/architecture firm, as an assistant to the designers who selected materials. My job was to obtain materials, or create them and style presentation boards. Then I grew into the role of special projects coordinator, oversaw site photography for magazine coverage of the firm and became the senior Specifications Writer for the company for finishes, selected all types of design products, determined which products the firm would maintain in its library as well as speak in trade shows for the firm and publish articles about design. Then ultimately I acquired the title Design Director of Interior finishes. Walker Group primarily produced retail design. It owned that market. The firm also worked on banks, hotels and restaurant projects. I was with this company for 29 years.

Grace: As an industry thought leader, what do you think we're doing great in this industry? What are we excelling in?

Steve: There's a cycle going on now that I applaud. That is a demise of the bean counters – very slow –but it's happening. So for example, Macys is finally doing a true renovation of their NY store. The company is now spending to redesign all of the interiors of their famous Herald Square flagship. A bean counter would allow only one department at a time or something small – but the bigger picture is more of a total environmental redo. Bloomingdales has long done that and has completed many total redo's in their family of stores, Lord and Taylor in NYC has instituted a significant renovation of its first floor with important work on all its other floors. Saks is committed too. When I worked on Saks in the 80s – the redo on the first floor, the most important floor, permitted the use of plastic laminate as a showcase base (a bean counter approach). That would never happen today. Saks is luxury all over. It's a different mindset.

Grace: What do you think we can improve upon as an industry?

Steve: We can improve on originality in retail. It touches many different things. There are thousands of examples for improvement. For example, I looked at the Christmas windows in Bloomingdales this year – most were beautiful, very simple – but there was one group of windows that took your picture when you got close up to them. The theme appeared to be: It's all about me. Apple recognized this ego idea when it created the "I phone" name years ago. Face books wants you "to like me." While fun – the concept plays to a long existing trend. Bloomingdales has a history of firsts. All the windows this past season should have been firsts.

Grace: If you can wave a magic wand and change one thing in our industry – what would it be?

Steve: I would like in the retail industry to celebrate quality; quality in product, quality in the expression of design and quality in comfort in shopping. It is very subjective but - it's a very busy, noisy loud experience in some places and it's purposely done that way – but if you want to focus and shop – there's a lot of distraction going on. People are used to that. I.e.: reading the news on the internet —stuff on the right, stuff on the left – very cluttered. By contrast – you go into an Apple stores and it's purposely designed so you focus on the product. They've achieved that, everything is simple so you see the product but that may not work on all environments.

Grace: Do you love what you do? How important do you feel it is for a leader – to absolutely love what they do?

Steve: I adore what I do! The problem I have with adoring what I do is that I have to learn to un-adore what I do so that I can accomplish something when I go into a store. Do I have to look at how two materials meet on an outside corner? Do I have to notice the color of light bulbs that are different because they didn't change them out consistently, do I have to notice grout lines? Macy's has a new jewelry department- beautiful stuff – I would soon as stand there and look at the marble, mosaic and finishes than actually go purchase the watch I'm looking for – it stops me in my tracks! Architecture and design wins and I often don't buy anything because of them, but I do have more money in the bank.

Grace: What are the top traits you feel make up strong Leadership?

Steve: A strong leader is an individual that has a real excellent competency and knowledge of what they are leading. With that comes personal security, the ability to take criticism, the ability to make fast decisions and the ability to work with people smarter than you. If you're going to be a good leader – you have to have not only good people around you – but the best people around you – no one can do it all. Being a leader is not telling someone what to do but working with them so they can make their own decisions – freeing you up to make other decisions.

Grace: What are the top traits you feel make up strong Teams?

Steve: A strong team would agree on a common goal that they really buy into. Each member would work towards the goal in his/her own way without feeling encumbered – a certain freedom to go your own way. They feel each other's support and just make it happen.

Grace: What is the most important lesson you've learned in this industry that will help someone else along their career path?

Steve: One's personal disposition and mix – it's the knowledge to know what you know and knowledge to know what you don't know. Assumptions out of the air don't work. A level of honestly for one's approach does. There are lots of people who keep their jobs because they are good at impressing others and therefore their average delivery is more than overlooked.

Grace: Who was the most impactful role model or mentor for you? How have they impacted your career? Your life?

Steve: When I was in 8th grade my history teacher Mr. Epstein made an important impact on my life. He was a nice person and made everyone laugh. However he was very insightful and told me he saw anger in me that I needed to resolve. At the time I had no idea what he meant. That has always stayed with me. As a young adult, I came to know what he meant in my college years, taking steps to resolve the anger I did not see. He was very influential – even after public school I maintained a friendship with him and his wife. Just that little seed planted in a few moments of an observation – saying something to me that I didn't understand, appreciate or denied, helped me years later.

Grace: Finish this sentence – one word that sums up my career's experiences in this industry and why that word.

Steve: One word that comes to mind – VARIED. The experiences I've had include having a gun to my head during a photo shoot. There was a fire that was set in the store where we were shooting and the police came. They thought I was setting the fires and literally had a gun to my head. When I told my boss – my boss asked "Did you photograph the 3rd floor?" I responded "Yes!" My boss said, "So what are you worried about?" In directing photography – I was given a set of plans and some points - take a shot here, take a shot there. But no further direction in going to a retailer store to pick what would be of interest not only to the firm but to the magazine. There are a zillion choices – but you have to pick the ones that magazines want to see. Also, picking the décor for FAO Schwartz - being responsible for the finishes to appeal to the public and the experience. In design you have color preferences. Years when reds are popular, then blues are popular, then the non committal grays! What do you do with this retailer that has every color of the rainbow? In this business having met and worked with many great leaders and figures like Mel Jacobs from Saks, they all had a strong vision and direction. Retailing was important – but stimulating – being playful, making shopping a memorable experience beyond product was key for them.

About Steve

As Director of Interior Finishes and senior associate for Walker Group CNI, Steve Kitezh has more than 25 years of experience in retail interior design specializing in department stores and specialty shops as well as public space design for condominiums, restaurants, and shopping malls. His work as a stylist/art director for site photography can be seen in many magazines such as Interior Design, VMSD, DDI and others. As a writer, he has been published in VMSD, DDI and Floor Covering News and has also presented at national and local conferences sponsored by DDI Magazine, NADI and ASID.

Steve's career includes work with many high end clients such as Bloomingdale's, FAO Schwarz, Saks Fifth Avenue, Rouse Corporation (Shops at National Place), Hyundai, Korean Life Insurance Co. and more. He was co-chairman of the committee to select the International store of the year for the Retail Design Institute, as well as the President of the NYC Chapter, and a judge for other design competitions. He is a "Fellow" of the Retail Design Institute, a certified speaker for the Architectural Woodworking Institute and a volunteer guest critic for The Fashion Institute of Technology and The Laboratory Institute for Merchandising.

CHAPTER 21

Inspiration

By Grace Daly

There are moments in our lives we clearly remember down to the smallest details. These are generally heartwarming or heart-wrenching pivotal moments that set the course of our life's path. This was one of my pivotal moments because someone believed in me.

It was 1990 on a warm summer day, and I was with my mom in her backyard. At full bloom, dozens of rosebushes, lush red tomatoes, firm green peppers and climbing vines of Chinese squash flourished all along the perimeter of this tiny backyard. There were large pots of succulent jade plants, as well as other auspicious plantings in various pots along the weathered concrete patio. My mom, with small silver clippers in hand, was trimming back the large potted plants of overgrown jasmine. This jasmine grew fragrantly wild, inviting you to come in close to the small white blossoms, close your eyes and deeply breathe in its soothing scent. "Mom, why are you cutting them down so much?" I asked. She responded, "When you cut down the stems, the blossoms will only grow back larger." I also remember being so sad on that perfect summer day. I had a sense of shame and humiliation when I first told my mom that I felt responsible for her losing her job just a few days earlier. To ease my pain, she calmly told me it was not my fault and that karma will take its course. My eyes filled with tears, and I turned away from her, pretending to squint from the glaring sun. I told her my dream of opening my own store one day, and I asked her if she believed I could do it. She whispered a response that resonated within my soul and proved true in the years ahead.

In the '80s I worked with a natural foods company in New York City's Tribeca. It was a good-size operation that had over 45,000 square feet of retail, wholesale and importing space. We were one of the first health food markets that carried organic vegetables, macrobiotic products, natural foods and natural health and beauty aids, as well as vitamins and supplements on a large scale. This was long before the general supermarket carried these types of products and long before there were natural foods chain stores. As general manager just barely in my twenties, I enjoyed a very lucrative salary and bonus structure. Having spent prior years in all positions—stock gal, cashier, buyer—it was a natural transition to grow into this senior management role, where I became acclimated with the wholesale and importing sides of the business as well as aspects in operations, visual merchandising and human resources. Aside from really enjoying what I did and being in an environment that encouraged healthy eating, there were many other perks: conference travel, unlimited access to both the corporate apartment in Battery Park City and the ski house in Vermont, and having an overview of every facet of the business. Still, the best benefit and one of my proudest moments ever in my career was when I got my mom a full-time job working in the retail store. I remember when I told her about my promotion and that I had already cleared it with the business owners to have her come aboard. She was so happy, she couldn't believe it. It would be the highest-paid salary she ever earned in her career and a much healthier work environment for her. She would be leaving her old job in the Chinatown sweatshops. This was long before seamstress jobs were outsourced to other countries, a time before there were proper safety and health regulations. The summers were brutally hot, with no air conditioning and only industrial metal fans that did little but to circulate the stifling heat, material fibers and dust. Some of the seamstress wore gauze masks over their noses and mouths to avoid breathing in these material fibers and the dust that permeated everything: your clothes, your hair. It caused discoloration under your fingernails, made your eyes itchy and your nose run the same color of the fabric you were sewing that week. The winters were equally cruel. They caused bleeding from dry, cracked fingers maneuvering rough denim material under the little metal arm of the dangerous sewing machine needle—the same needles that would pierce tender fingers and thumbs of the novice seamstress.

At the retail store, my mom flourished. Her English improved with an expanding vocabulary to include the many various names of organic produce, Japanese food products and other natural foods. As the unofficial store "mom," she resurrected the old kitchen area in the warehouse, where she whipped up huge vats of organic miso soup or prepared fresh salads, ensuring that the store employees ate well during their breaks. Everyone on the team loved her, expressing their gratitude with a hug or kiss on her cheek after they ate: "Thank you, Susie Mommy." The regular customers and nannies with the stroller babies sought her warm smile upon entering the store each day. Knowing my mom was in a great working environment allowed to me take care of business. I was crazy busy running around, unloading trucks, moving pallets of shipment off the loading dock, working the cable run freight elevators, redirecting the warehouse, placing merchandise orders, taking wholesale orders, getting payroll in and supporting the team goals each day. My mom would always look for me during the day to make sure I stopped to eat lunch. Once in a while she'd plead with me when she saw me maneuvering heavy pallets of grains. "You should not be doing that. You may pull something and not be able to bear children when you get older!" I'd shout back over my shoulder, "It's no big deal! It's all in leveraging the weight and momentum!" My mom was an integral part of the store's spirit and energy. Having had the opportunity to work with her those years helped me understand and develop a compassion and genuine care for my team members. These very core leadership traits would propel my future career in retail development.

After several years of my mom working at the store, one day it all changed. Simply put, the owner was getting a divorce and the business was bought out by his ex-wife. She ran the business with her new partner who owned a trucking company, and it was evident that major changes were already in motion. The shelves became thin, with only one or two facings deep of product. Music wasn't allowed on the sales floor, the warehouse, the loading dock or anywhere else anymore. The employees' hours were cut back just enough to keep them out of a full-time status to avoid providing benefits. No matter how hard the staff worked, it was never enough to earn a simple thank-you or a smile. Everything the managers did was questioned. Everything I did was scrutinized. Tired of working in fear under this tyranny, a few team members walked out, while the rest slipped into the heavy dark gloom that hung over the store. The customers immediately sensed the change in the store's energy, and sales dropped dramatically. Realizing that there was nothing more I could contribute to in a positive manner—and as hard as it was—I decided it was my time to leave, too. My only concern was that I would leave my mom in such a poor, unhappy environment. I met with the new owners and offered my two weeks' notice. I was careful to be politically correct in my approach, informing them that I wanted to pursue my college education full-time. I thanked them for my time with the company and the opportunity to learn everything I did. They were cold and expressionless. With blank stares, they plainly instructed me to take my mother with me when I leave in two weeks. I couldn't believe it. That was the hardest thing I ever had to do. I had to tell my mother she lost her job. I have always felt as responsible for her losing this job as I felt responsible for her initial opportunity in having this job. I cried when I told my mother the news. I told her I am sorry she lost her job because of the new owners' malicious egos over my choosing to leave the company.

Within a year, I heard through the industry grapevine of the insidious demise of their business. One morning, store employees showed up to an empty and padlocked store. Apparently the new owners had packed up the entire store overnight with all their trucks and tractor-trailers. All the merchandise, the shelves, the fixtures, and the equipment were gone. They left countless suppliers with open invoices, as well as the employees without their last two weeks of pay. Just like that, they were gone. When my mother heard the news, she said she was glad she was not there until the end; to have to endure such a negative environment was one thing, but then to get stiffed for two weeks' pay was the kicker. Needless to say, these business owners were not kind people. I don't doubt that they have been paying their karmic debt ever since. This was my first experience with poor "leadership," very bad business practices and very bad people. Still, it taught me an invaluable lesson about how to treat people with love and respect because it's their dedication that drives our businesses. It's always about the people. The product and processes are secondary because our people create this energy to drive the products and drive the processes. It became ingrained in me to never lead with ego; never lead from that dark place of fear and scarcity. This experience confirmed in me that I could still learn the best lessons even from the worst people.

Back to my mom and me in her backyard, trimming those beautiful overgrown jasmine bushes on a warm summer day. I was burdened with the shame and sense of responsibility I felt with her losing her job. She calmly replied that karma will take its course, as it always does. "Mom, do you believe one day I will open a retail store?" She stopped pruning the jasmines and looked right at me. What she whispered next would resonate with my soul and prove to be true in the years ahead: "Of course, I believe you will. But you won't just open one store; you'll open hundreds and hundreds of stores throughout the country."

Within a few years of that fateful summer day in my mom's backyard, I was on the construction team with Blockbuster Entertainment, going gangbusters with an aggressive new store rollout program. In one record year we opened over 600 Blockbuster Video stores throughout the country. That's where I learned the store opening business as a project coordinator in the northeast construction department: learning to read plans, doing takeoffs, ordering flooring, lighting, fixtures and cash wraps while assisting my construction project managers. Like a little sister, I tagged along to construction sites with my PMs every time I could, diligently asking questions and taking note of how my PMs spoke with respect, gratitude and the spirit of partnership to the super and tradesman on site. I made a few mistakes along the way, owned up to them and corrected them, said "please" and "thank you" as often as I could, and ultimately learned the development business hands-on. Since then, my career has led me to other retailers where I directed value engineering and prototype design, new store construction and facilities maintenance for national retail chains, including Noodle Kidoodle, Vitamin World, Ann Taylor and Equinox Fitness. My twenty years of experience in the retail development track has indeed resulted in well over 700 new stores and thousands of remodels, refreshes, retrofits and repair maintenance projects nationwide. Granted, I do not own these stores; it is not my company—but this thriving career has afforded me the opportunities of travel and luxury with my family and parents. I have worked with some of the most incredible people in this industry (including my co-authors in this book) and have been fortunate enough to have amazing mentors throughout my career and also conversely to be a mentor to many team members and industry colleagues. Now operating from an independent platform, my successes have reached new heights. As a coach, author, speaker, industry columnist and show host, I am living in fulfillment and authenticity to my purpose. My purpose and path are in helping to shine a spotlight on all the great people in this industry that I grew up in. This is all because in my darkest hour, on a warm summer's day in my mother's garden, she cared and believed in me deeply and planted this seed with her wisdom. This inception ultimately launched my lifelong career and passion for this industry. She never gave up on me, even though at that point in my life, I had almost given up on myself. For this and many other reasons, I am eternally grateful to my mom. She infused a belief and trust in me that everything will not just work out, but my career, my life will flourish in ways I could not even imagine. I have always remembered this and have strived hard to provide the same support and inspiration to my son, loved ones and my very dear friends and colleagues in this industry.

About Grace

Grace Daly is a certified coach, award-winning writer, international bestselling author, inspirational speaker and industry columnist. She is the founder, master interviewer and host of *ShopTalk Evolution*, the Industry's internet radio talk show focusing on retail and restaurant development in the brick-and-mortar world. Grace's published books include *The Seven Success Keys for the Retail Facilities Professional: The Ultimate Guide to the Fulfillment of Your Career, Everyday Inspiration,* and co-author to the bestsellers *Win: 35 Winning Strategies from Today's Leading Entrepreneurs, The Only Business Book You'll Ever Need* (with Brian Tracy), and *The Success Secret* (with Jack Canfield). Combining her passion for writing and coaching, Grace is the founder of Well of Strength. Well of Strength is a non-profit organization to help Americans overcome challenging life events through the power of writing.

Grace's 20+ years in the retail design, construction and facilities industry have demonstrated a successful track record in directing aggressive store development programs, open remodels and facilities management. Her experience embraces the custom details of luxury brands and the volume demands of national multi-unit chains, covering properties from 2k to 50k square feet.

Grace has participated on multiple panels and moderated roundtable discussions, and has served on the following industry boards: SPECS Advisory Board 2001, 2002; PRSM Executive Board Member 2002, 2003, Education Committee & Board Nominating Committee; NYC Chapter ISP member 2002-2005; and the Editorial Board of *Retail Construction Magazine* 2005-2009. Grace is the recipient of several awards and honors, including 2012/2013 NAPW Professional Women of the

Year, 2011 and 2012 Best-Sellers' Quilly Awards from the National Academy of Best-Selling Authors, and the 2011 and 2012 Editor's Choice Awards. She is also a member of the National Academy of Best-Selling Authors and The American Society of Journalists and Authors. Grace's work has been seen on *USA Today*, the PBS television network, and the Guggenheim Museum and Kenny Gallery.

A passionate advocate for the advancement and recognition of the retail and restaurant development industry, Grace also partners with diverse organizations to mentor and empower groups in various stages of their careers to take action toward fulfilling their dreams. Get Ready, Get Inspired!®

33 5 AH Road

- Tony -
6 am